Contents

	FOREWORD	5
1	My name is Gabriel	8
2	Everyday autism	10
3	'Sweet are the uses of adversity', or every stick has two ends	25
4	More life and times on Planet Autism	40
5	'When did you know?'	51
6	A cuckoo in the nest	61
7	New school	71
8	Growing up, or fitting a square peg into a round hole	81
9	'But the greatest of these is charity'	92
10	Many happy returns of the day	106
11	Cousin Mary, Victor of Aveyron and Peter the Wild Boy	124
12	Autism: What is it? What causes it? What can be done about it?	139
13	'Of my life story I know only the middle, not the beginning nor the end'	155
14	Dark days	165
15	Shit happens	175
16	Turkeys don't cry	185
17	A free spirit	194
	LIST OF QUOTATIONS	206

For my mother,
and my sons
Christian, Gabriel and Jacob

Growing Up Severely Autistic
They Call Me Gabriel

Kate Rankin

Jessica Kingsley Publishers
London and Philadelphia

First published in the United Kingdom in 2000 by
Jessica Kingsley Publishers Ltd,
116 Pentonville Road, London
N1 9JB, England

and

325 Chestnut Street,
Philadelphia, PA 19106, USA.

www.jkp.com

Library of Congress Cataloging in Publication Data

A CIP Catalog record for this book is available from the Library of Congress

British Library Cataloguing in Publication Data

A CIP Catalogue record for this book is available from the British Library

ISBN 1 85302 891 6

Printed and Bound in Great Britain by
Athenaeum Press, Gateshead, Tyne and Wear

Foreword

A few years ago I wrote an article about Gabriel, my son, in which I referred to him as an 'idiot'. I used the word not as an insult but to convey just how handicapped and utterly helpless he was. I explained: 'He does not speak, has very little understanding of language, no sense of danger, is obsessive, hyperactive and still shits in his pants.' I wasn't surprised that some readers objected to my use of the word; nowadays it is all right to call idiot someone who is *not* — your husband, friend, child — but it is not all right to use it about someone like my son.

In the world of mental disorder terms are constantly changing. Words that at one time were terms of reference have fallen out of favour or become terms of abuse; we no longer refer to a group of people as idiots, imbeciles, half-wits or mental defectives. Nor do we now describe such people as feeble minded, retarded or subnormal. Even in Gabriel's lifetime terms have been changed; he and his peers were described as being 'mentally handicapped' a few years ago but that expression is now no longer current — or more precisely, correct. Yesterday's idiot is today's 'person with learning difficulties'.

The new descriptions reflect new attitudes and are an attempt to give respect and dignity to these, our fellow human beings; to do away with discrimination and accord them their rights. Thankfully those grim days have passed when the public would visit such places as the Bethlem Hospital on a Sunday afternoon to laugh at and make sport of the miserable inhabitants; experts no longer argue over whether 'idiots are truly human'. Nevertheless it is not so long ago that many mentally handicapped people spent their lives in the wards of huge institutions, their days dull and regimented and with little respect paid to their privacy, individuality or even humanity. Gabriel's generation is fortunate to have been born as the pendulum has started to swing towards, we hope, a more enlightened approach

– and after all how a society treats its sick and disabled is a good indicator of how civilized that society is.

Unfortunately when this enlightenment is overlaid with political correctness it can result in what could be considered mealy-mouthed euphemism. Who couldn't admit to having a few 'learning difficulties', even 'severe' ones? (Setting the video, for example.) The words include a whole melting pot of conditions and disabilities from people severely brain damaged and physically disabled to the dyslexic – as does the term 'special needs', another all-encompassing, non-specific expression.

The point is that probably for the majority of people with learning difficulties it does not make a great deal of difference what words we use – it certainly doesn't as far as Gabriel is concerned. Besides it is not what we call them, but how we call them that is important. I have therefore used a mixture of terms. As I have said, my generation grew up with the expression mentally handicapped and many continue to use it (though apt, its disadvantage is to be confused with mentally ill, often by those who should know better); I have also referred to people with learning difficulties or disabilities or special needs. No doubt in time these expressions too will fall into disrepute and be superseded by others.

As for the word 'autistic', which was only coined in the 1940s to define a particular group of children with certain characteristics, that too is no longer the officially accepted term. Professionals in the field of autism prefer to talk about 'people with autism' or 'people with autistic spectrum disorders' – ASD for short – since the disorder is now considered to cover a far wider range than originally thought. However, for the sake of simplicity and since it is the word people are most familiar with, I have mostly described Gabriel and people like him as autistic. (Not to be confused with 'artistic' – which happens.)

Above all it is necessary to remember that we are talking about individuals. People with learning difficulties or with autism or both include as wide a range and variety of people as those who do not suffer from these problems, and equally have their own personalities and characters. They are people in their own right who, most importantly, show us there are many ways of being human. Perhaps we should bear in mind that the original meaning of 'idiot' was a person who was unique in a way that others are not – and Gabriel is certainly that.

Finally, this is a personal account of my son's life and his impact on the family. Readers will almost certainly disagree with some of my views, and no doubt we have made many mistakes in the way we have dealt with our situation. For those faults I have only myself to blame, and I hope both readers and Gabriel will forgive me.

Note

Although I have made several references to the National Autistic Society (NAS) and its magazine *Communication*, the views and opinions in these pages are my own and not necessarily those held by the NAS. For those seeking further information or help please contact the NAS:

The National Autistic Society
393 City Road
London EC1V 1NG
Tel: 020 7833 2299

My name is Gabriel

He is called Gabriel, he is 15, autistic and severely mentally handicapped. He's an *enfant sauvage*, a wild child.

Gabriel has no spoken language; equally his understanding of language is very rudimentary. He understands such simple phrases as 'Tea's ready' or 'Sit down' or 'We're going out in the car', though he probably only recognises such words as 'tea' or 'car' and guesses the rest, while at other times he appears to have completely forgotten the meaning of the most familiar phrase. It was several years before he knew *he* was Gabriel.

On the other hand he has no difficulty in expressing and obtaining his basic needs – food, music, clean pants, a bath or a walk. This he does by taking the nearest hand – anybody's, mine, his father's, or that of one of his brothers – and pulling the hand to the required object. The peanut butter, the CD player, the front door. Of course we're used to his wants by now and can anticipate them and we ask him 'Do you want a bath, Gabriel? Say "please" if you do' and then he touches his lips with his hand (the one sign he has acquired in twelve years of schooling) which we take to mean 'yes'.

Frequently however he cannot be bothered to ask, he just takes, and he is especially adroit at stealing food. He can have something off your fork or off the supermarket shelf and into his mouth with the speed of light. And although we say 'no' very firmly and we think he knows he shouldn't do these things, he doesn't really know *why* he shouldn't – so he carries on doing them anyway. Similarly he doesn't know why he shouldn't eat the discarded chips he sees lying in the gutter or drink from a half-empty bottle he's spotted in a refuse bin. He doesn't care.

Gabriel can't play Beethoven by ear or draw cathedrals; he can't even spread a piece of bread or wash his face — he's just not interested. His main interest is twirling and flapping, with a bit of tearing thrown in. For this he favours grasses, shoelaces, tissues or, just now, that bright orange tape workmen use to tie around scaffolding and roadworks, which he collects on our walks. Sometimes his remorseless pursuit of this activity becomes like the dripping tap of Chinese torture for those who live with him, though more disturbing are his explosive moods, when he rages and screams and slaps himself.

Physically Gabriel is extremely — alarmingly — able. He runs, climbs and jumps fearlessly, can wriggle through the smallest aperture and swim like a fish, all of which lead to difficulties of a different nature and he needs to be watched constantly. Despite his daring however he rarely hurts himself, though that might be more due to his apparent imperviousness to pain.

As far as people are concerned Gabriel doesn't take a lot of notice of them. He prefers things. It is true he is quite curious if new people come to the house and often likes to smell them or touch their hair, but he's not too keen on approaching them. He's also very averse to looking anyone in the eyes, though that is not to say he is un-observant. He can scan a room in an instant and spot something new or different, or — especially — something that has been put out of his reach in the hope he won't notice it.

Many of Gabriel's ways are odd and idiosyncratic — such as his insistence on sleeping downstairs in the kitchen/diner rather than his bedroom. He doesn't seem to mind the hard floor (perhaps he feels more secure close to the ground?) or the draught from the back door. There is quite a large broom cupboard in the corner of the room where he keeps his twirling collection which he seems to think of as his space, and he likes to sleep there wrapped in his duvet, with his head in the cupboard next to his twirlers.

Everyday autism

Saturday 22 January

In the morning we took Gabriel down the town to be socialised; we took him shopping in other words.

We live a short distance from the high street so we walk there, then through the market and into one or two shops before returning home. We keep it simple and Neil watches Gabriel while I do the buying; the whole outing takes about an hour.

Aim number one is to learn to WAIT in shops and NOT TO GRAB. This is extremely difficult for him, but constant dripping wears a stone and he knows the routine and is generally happy to come with us.

A liking for routine and sameness is a definite feature of autism and many autistic people insist on adhering rigidly to their routines – the order they put their clothes on or how the table is laid, for example. (Of course many normal people like routine too. It is a matter of degree.) It is not uncommon for some children to scream and throw tantrums at the least alteration in these routines – if say a different route is taken to the shops – and this can make life very difficult for their families. Fortunately for us Gabriel is not like this, but we feel routine is valuable in giving some structure to his day.

He bursts out of the house when we open the door, dashes off to snatch some grasses from the roadside to fiddle with before settling down to a steady trot. We go into the supermarket first (something we normally avoid for we cannot try his patience too far) and he attempts to climb into a trolley. Fifteen years old and he still likes a ride. Neil succeeds in deflecting him with a mention of biscuits – not very subtle I admit – and he drags us to the confectionery department, chooses a packet of jam tarts and rips it open instantly to start on the contents.

Back in the street he strides along not looking to right or left. He hasn't a clue how to behave. Two friends stand on the pavement talking together; Gabriel walks between them. They look furious and we catch mutterings about 'badly brought up children'. A woman is gazing in a shop window; he pushes between her and the window. She looks surprised for a moment but then realises he's not 'normal'. We try to anticipate these situations and steer him clear. Neil spots a toddler in a pushchair sucking a comforter – a favourite target – and gets ready in case he makes a grab for it, similarly when we see a little girl with a balloon. 'Come on Gabriel, we'll buy you some balloons to play with over the weekend.' Then passing through the market, in spite of Neil's vigilance he manages to snatch a handful of grapes. I apologise helplessly to the stallholder but he brushes my apologies aside, 'That's alright love, don't you worry. Here, give him these.' And he hands over a small bag of loose ones. Perhaps he recognises us from our weekly expeditions or maybe he has a handicapped relative or neighbour himself and knows what it's about. People vary enormously in their reactions to these incidents.

I take the grapes gratefully and we continue to the baker's. For once the Wild Boy behaves very well and with not too much difficulty is persuaded not to grab an iced bun from the window immediately but to wait for the assistant and to proffer the money. This he does without apparently having the remotest idea why; he does it rather like a performing animal, simply because that is what he is required to do to get the reward. No doubt he showed reasonable self-control as he had already had several jam tarts and the grapes; nevertheless we tell him what a good boy he has been and head for home.

Quite a successful morning really; no outbursts or difficult incidents and we are especially pleased about the baker's. It's the first time he has done that.

So what do people see when they look at Gabriel?

Unlike a child with say Down's syndrome, Gabriel's handicap is not immediately recognisable or even apparent. Many autistic children look normal and frequently they are very good-looking. I thought Gabriel was quite beautiful as an infant and was perplexed when first we began to worry about him saying, 'But he doesn't *look* handicapped, he doesn't look stupid.' As the children get older their appearance tends to become odder, their gestures more pronounced, and this has been true of Gabriel also; nonetheless at first glance many adults are often not aware that he is not normal. (It is interesting that children are much more observant and invariably notice something strange about Gabriel the moment they set eyes on him – and they have no inhibitions about their curiosity.)

Age 14

They see then quite a handsome, slim, healthy-looking boy with thick dark hair and large brown eyes. They would probably be surprised to find he is 15 as he appears to be two or three years younger, both in his face and in his build. If they look a little longer they might notice that those beautiful eyes lack the responsiveness that one expects in another human being and that there is a certain emptiness behind them. The main clues to his condition though are in his gestures, his manner, his behaviour. They see an adolescent whose whole attention is concentrated on some leaves or a length of string he is holding in his hands, who only looks up fleetingly, who hurries along, head bent over, seemingly unaware of his surroundings. When his parents stop to make their purchases they see him sit cross-legged on the pavement or shop floor and when they speak to him he doesn't reply. No, they conclude, he's definitely not normal.

Sunday 23 January

Gabriel was very tired all morning and kept trying to doze on the sofa. Like everything else about him, his sleeping is very erratic, try as we might to establish a regular pattern with him. As far as we know he slept all night so shouldn't be tired. Can he be ill then? He's rather like an animal when he's not well – just curls up in a corner and sleeps. And as with an animal one can only look for symptoms. He can't tell us what is wrong – but what is more, he won't let us near him to examine him properly or take his temperature. (Whatever would we do if he were seriously ill? Luckily he's a robust child.) Still, what to do this morning? If he's not ill we'd better wake him or he'll be up all night – and so will we. As we hesitate he slowly comes to life. He gets more and more lively as the day proceeds until he is into his usual activity of running back and forth with his twirlers and is so busy running through the house at one time that he pees in his pants. He doesn't appear to care or even notice. I change him but he decides he doesn't want to get dressed again and spends the evening in his underpants. Dirties four pairs before bedtime – ours that is; he is roaring around full of beans at midnight. How foolish of me to have imagined he was ill; I should have known better. We leave him to it and sleep in the spare room where we can't hear him so much.

School tomorrow. Hooray!

Monday 24 January

I start attempting to wake Gabriel at 7.15. It's as difficult to wake him as it is to get him to sleep especially if, as this morning, he has had only three or four hours sleep. He sees no reason why he should wake and it's only our habitual harrying of many years that finally convinces him it's useless to resist and forces him to his feet and into the bathroom.

Change his nappy – it's invariably dirty and a lovely job before breakfast – then wash him. Yes, it's true, he can't even wash himself. Of course this is something they try to teach him at school. Handed a flannel and encouraged he might wipe his face cursorily – but the action appears to have no meaning for him, he doesn't seem to make any connection. Given the soap and told to wash his hands, Gabriel is more interested in gouging out nailfuls of soap and rubbing it on the windows or eating it rather than using it for its intended purpose. We too try to teach him the basics of self-care but time is short in the mornings on school days.

Time to get dressed next. Gabriel can dress himself – in a fashion – but if his trousers or sweatshirt are not on back to front or inside out it is by chance rather than intention. Socks are pulled on with the heels on the top of the instep and there's a fifty-fifty chance that his shoes will be on the wrong feet. It's all the same to him. He doesn't care. Still I don't want him to go off to school looking as if he's been dragged through a hedge backwards, so I help him put his clothes on, prompting and coaxing and pointing out the labels to help him know back from front. (It's bound to 'click' one day, isn't it?) But it's uphill all the way with Gabriel and while I look for a pair of clean socks he lies down and falls asleep again. Never mind, nearly there, just tie his laces and tell him to sit at the table for breakfast while I write in his book.

This is his home/school book which goes with him, with any relevant information staff might like or need to know. I tell them about giving the money in the baker's; also that he has had very little sleep but we would be grateful if they could keep him awake at school and that he has had a happy and (relatively) stable weekend.

The taxi and escort arrive at 8.30 to take Gabriel – he has the same school hours and holidays as normal children and we are very fortunate that he attends a school specifically for autistic children. Since in common with many of the other children he is mute, we rely on the escort to pass messages back and forth, as well as sending the book at the beginning of the week, to be returned on Friday. In the meantime Gabriel has removed his shoes and is asleep again. Nuisance! If only he would fall asleep that promptly at night. But it's all right, Tom, his escort who is coaxing him into the taxi ('Come along now, darling') has a duster ready for him to play with on the journey – they keep it in the taxi – and he soon goes off happily. 'Goodbye Gabes, see you later.' But he doesn't respond or even look at us as they drive away; he's busy with his duster and I breathe a sigh of relief at the prospect of eight Gabriel-free hours as the taxi disappears.

They pass all too quickly though and the 4 o'clock deadline is soon hovering over me. (Must get that done before HE gets home.) Shortly before he's due back I make sure the bedroom doors are locked. He is likely to climb out of windows or interfere with things – tear posters, pull tapes out of cassettes or turn plants out of their pots or – well, just about anything a curious or mischievous toddler might do. I lock the windows downstairs that open onto the street and put away anything I've been using that might attract him – polish, paint, papers, sewing, etc. He generally arrives home in top gear, rushing through the house like a whirlwind and one can't be too careful. A pot of glue, say, inadvertently left on the table would have a hand stuck in it and glue would be everywhere before I had even said goodbye to the escort. I put away food and lock the kitchen cupboards and finally make sure the garden gate is securely fastened. I try to be prepared so that when he arrives I can offer him something to eat and join him with a cup of tea without suddenly finding he has discovered an open window or is having fun with a bottle of shampoo.

Fairly quiet this afternoon. After demolishing a bowl of cereal he even lay down on the sofa – something absolutely unheard of when he was younger however little sleep he had had – but having stoked up at tea he got more and more lively as the evening passed so that by half-past midnight he was wide awake.

We slept in the spare room again.

Tuesday 25 January

Skidded across the kitchen on pieces of orange peel when I went to wake our Madcap this morning. He had eaten an orange during the night and then torn the peel into dozens of minute fragments. One of Gabriel's 'skills' is an ability to make the most amount of mess with the least amount of material. Must remember to remove the fruit bowl in future.

Very tired this afternoon after school and no wonder, has only slept about seven hours since Sunday. He couldn't wait to have his bath and go to bed and was tucked up and asleep by 9.30. Lovely. A nice quiet evening.

Wednesday 26 January

Just as we were going to bed last night we heard Gabriel having a fit in his sleep.

Poor Gabriel, he suffers from epilepsy – not uncommon with autistic people – and a week rarely passes without at least one fit. Luckily he almost always fits in his sleep these days so we needn't be too worried about falls or fitting in the bath or swimming pool. Nevertheless we must always be alert and though I must have witnessed hundreds of fits by now I still find it upsetting and never get used to seeing his eyes roll up and his lips turn blue as he shakes uncontrollably from head to toe. Each seizure lasts only two or three minutes but it always seems much longer.

So no school today as we know from experience he will need to spend most of the day sleeping it off, and since I won't be able to get out of the house I take the opportunity to clean out his cupboard. It contained the following 'toys':

About 12 assorted laces, including a shocking pink pair (Xmas present from cousin)

1 tie, very ragged

1 scarf, very grubby

1 torch, batteries dead. Must buy more – but they rarely last more than a day

1 tea-strainer, which he used to like balancing on his head

1 wriggly snake, from school trip to zoo

1 curly key-ring, another present from a cousin

1 quality wooden baby's toy, present from his brother Jacob aged 11, who bought it because quote: it will fascinate any child of 18 months and is virtually indestructible

Plus assorted dusters, dish-cloths, tea-towels and fluorescent tape

I try with great difficulty to keep him awake from lunchtime on. Later in the afternoon when Neil gets home he takes him for a walk to keep him on his feet, but he stumbles along like a zombie and spends the rest of the day snoozing until we let him go to bed at 10 pm. An 'easy' day, but we'll pay for this tomorrow.

Thursday 27 January

Very withdrawn when woken this morning. Glowering and head-banging. The headbanging doesn't appear to hurt him but it can turn a little violent and on one occasion he broke a double-glazed window with his head. Didn't want breakfast. Gabriel usually seems 'hung-over' after a fit, not surprisingly, and somewhat disorientated, so I did feel rather bad about sending him to school as I expected him to be difficult. To be honest I just couldn't face a day of screaming and headbanging – at least at school there are several of them to look after him. I needn't have worried, he's so changeable it turned out he was 'as good as gold all day', so Tom reported when he delivered him in the afternoon.

Very lively all evening and most of the night. Again. (Another reason for sending him to school – I knew what was coming.) Because he slept so much yesterday he isn't tired today and tonight. Gabriel often doesn't go to sleep until 3 or 4 am or later, and regularly – about once a week – stays up all night and is still full of energy the following day. His body clock is utterly dysfunctional.

Of course now our son insists on sleeping downstairs we have to take certain precautions before we go to bed when Gabriel is about to have a late night. As he likes playing with water we turn it off at the mains so that he can't leave the taps running all night or flood the kitchen. We also remove fuses so that he doesn't stay up flicking the lights on and off, and so that hopefully the darkness will encourage sleep. Check of course that doors and windows are locked as well as the kitchen cupboards. (Neil fitted locks on all the food cupboards after an incident one night with a bag of flour – I won't go into details!) We remove any papers that might be in the room – £10 notes, etc. – that could be shredded by morning. Remove fruit bowl too now, then lock him in and hope for the best; hope he just wanders about quietly until he is ready for sleep and doesn't run up and down shrieking and laughing. We are uneasily aware that he is awake and sleep fitfully until peace finally descends.

This might seem like a lot of trouble – it *is a* lot of trouble – but to have Gabriel thumping about all night in an adjacent bedroom is, if anything, even more disturbing. Fortunately, once asleep he never wakes, the problem is getting there. However broken nights and lack of sleep are facts of life for most families with handicapped children, in some cases with far-reaching and devastating effects.

Friday 28 January

Gabriel was so tired this morning he could hardly keep his eyes open during breakfast and kept laying his head down on the table; he had evidently not fallen asleep till late. I sent him to school anyway hoping he would come to in the taxi.

11 am: Call from school to say he couldn't be woken. I knew if I didn't go and fetch him he would sleep the rest of the day and be up

all night again so drove 14 miles to school, brought him home, gave him a cup of coffee – industrial strength – and put him in the garden. He woke quite easily and then spent a happy afternoon running around and blowing bubbles.

Blowing bubbles is one of Gabriel's favourite activities. He often asks for a bowl of water with some washing-up liquid in and then blows down a plastic tube into it – or sucks it up and drinks it. In fact he usually ends up drinking most of it as he especially likes the taste of soapy water – often scooping up handfuls of it to drink when the sink is full of washing up, much to the amazement and disgust of visitors. He is also very partial to neat washing-up liquid and shampoo and will take great swigs of them, which is why they are kept under lock and key. He then walks around frothing at the lips.

Changed several pairs of dirty pants (we take it in turns). Seem to have changed endless pairs the last few days – though no doubt a dose of washing-up liquid doesn't help to limit the bowel movements – and wonder if it will ever end.

When Gabriel was about 4 years old I met a woman with an autistic son and was horrified to hear that he hadn't learnt to use the lavatory until he was 17. Seventeen! And now my own son is approaching 16 and seems hardly nearer to being toilet trained than he was then.

Had a little altercation over a credit card during the evening. He had taken it out of Neil's wallet to play with although this is not allowed as he likes to snap them in half. (Scene in bank, to uncomprehending cashier: Yes, I know this is the fourth card I've had this year but my teenage son keeps breaking them.) Was furious when it was taken away and jumped up and down shouting and thumping his chest 'Just like a gorilla,' observed Christian his older brother, who has always enjoyed nature programmes.

Monday 31 January – Friday 4 February

This whole week has been taken up with autism – by that I mean activities, appointments and functions connected with Gabriel. At 15 his future is looming – he has to leave his present school at 16, this July in fact, and wheels have been turning for a year or so already.

Although we feel Gabriel should go into residential care eventually – in three or four years' time perhaps – we would like him to continue living at home for the time being. This means finding somewhere within about thirty miles of home and to that end there have been consultations with the careers officer (yes, that's what they call her, and part of her brief is to help find a place for Gabriel), social worker, headmistress and half a dozen other assorted professionals.

Just before Christmas we learnt that the school we had been hoping Gabriel would transfer to for the next three years, until he was 19, would not accept him. They felt they could not manage him and because of his escaping habit were worried about security. We did not dispute their decision but we were very angry that it had taken seven months from our first visit and application for a place to the final refusal, leaving us very little time to look elsewhere.

(I must just add here that towards the end of this saga – for that's what it turned out to be – it was arranged for Gabriel to spend three days at this school for a final assessment of his suitability. Imagine our dismay when we took him there and found that the staff were expecting a child in a wheelchair and had therefore put him in a group of very fragile and vulnerable children. This was after months of form filling, explanations, descriptions and extensive input from ourselves, his teachers and social worker. Sometimes one does despair.)

Well, there is not a lot of choice for the Gabriels of this world (or their parents), and when I rang choice number two to make enquiries I laid it on the line right at the start: our son was autistic with 'challenging behaviour'. Challenging behaviour covers behaviour that is confrontational, aggressive, disruptive or demanding constant attention. Bloody difficult in other words – and all these descriptions apply to Gabriel except that he is not (gratuitously) aggressive. On the other hand his constant desire to escape presents serious problems for all his carers. This escaping propensity is not uncommon in autistic children and his present school is surrounded by a high fence and doors and windows are kept locked. However, the height of the fence didn't deter Gabriel from trying to get out and at one time he had to wear a cowbell in the playground (until a new teacher removed it, considering it undignified). I explained all this to the

Head and was delighted to be told he would never exclude anyone on the grounds of challenging behaviour and an appointment was made for this Monday.

Neil is a self-employed carpenter and joiner so he is able to accompany me on these occasions. It is not so easy for many fathers or indeed mothers who are employed to take time off for the frequent appointments we have to attend with doctors, teachers, psychiatrists, social workers, therapists and all the others. Many employers do not take kindly to constant requests for time off, even when pay is deducted from wage packets. Many parents feel that professionals do not appreciate the fact that they are being paid to attend meetings, whereas parents are often forfeiting money or holiday time in order to attend the same meeting – meetings which are often cancelled, start late, or concerning issues about which those involved are not properly informed. On this occasion however the appointment had to be cancelled at the last minute by ourselves: Gabriel had a fit and it had to be postponed to the following day.

So the three of us went there on Tuesday. The college, for so it is called, is situated in the grounds of what was formerly a large hospital for the mentally ill which, with the new 'care in the community' policy, was being dismantled and redeveloped. Some of the class-rooms were in an old church that stood on the site. We had been warned that the buildings and surroundings could be off-putting but we were not too discouraged by the old-fashioned 'institutional' blocks. What was more important in our view was that we very much liked the Head and felt there was a good atmosphere and a sense of renewal pervading the place. Even the old church seemed quite cosy. At one end of it a group of students were preparing elevenses in their fashion, and we were offered drinks and biscuits which we enjoyed while dodging flying biros targeted by one student at the teacher, who however appeared fairly blasé: 'Take no notice, he's just doing it to get attention. Mind you, he's got a deadly aim' – and he ducked again. Another quickly helped himself to an extra six spoonfuls of sugar while the teacher's attention was momentarily diverted and Gabriel, who has an unerring eye for a biscuit tin, was making inroads into their week's supply.

We needed to check how secure the place was – at least it stood in several acres and there were no busy roads nearby. There was a small recreation area surrounded by a fence that wouldn't really pose much of a problem to our boy but we and they felt, perhaps a trifle optimistically, that with adequate supervision Gabriel could be contained. We decided to apply for a place. He could go there in September and stay there indefinitely, giving us time to settle future plans and find a long-term residential home.

Let's hope this application goes more smoothly than the last.

Wednesday night was Parent Teachers Association meeting. I joined the PTA when Gabriel joined the school. Working with children as difficult and demanding as ours requires dedication and effort on the part of the teachers way beyond the limits of duty. Many of the staff work and give their time unstintingly and they deserve and need the support of the parents. Of course the school always needs funds like any other and raising them is one of the main objectives of the PTA; as a member I am directly helping my child. Added to that it is an excellent way to keep up to date with developments and plans (of course we get no news from Gabriel), as well as an opportunity to meet other parents and staff. To tell the truth there is also an element of self-interest – we hope teachers will be more sympathetic to ourselves and Gabriel because of our participation. (Neil's contribution consists of mending the school bikes in the holidays. All of them get totally wrecked every term!)

There is the usual planning of fund-raising events and allocation of funds already raised – new tape recorders, bikes, holidays, and so on. Lots of interesting gossip and boring banter all for the good of the cause.

Thursday morning to local support group. An informal get-together of mums of mentally handicapped children. We meet about once a month in each other's homes and though we occasionally have a visitor from the educational or social services or a speaker on some relevant subject, we mostly spend the time talking about our children, their problems and progress. Of course we have a lot to say about the services provided and all the professionals we come in contact with and I'm afraid our comments are not always very complimentary. We've seen too much, had too many shiftings of goal posts, reorganising of services and redeploying of personnel. From time to time when we have been very dissatisfied with something as a group we have been able to exert some pressure – and even get a result.

I have found it a great support and an invaluable help on a practical level. This morning I ask if anyone knows anything about the college we visited on Tuesday and hear a glowing account from one mother whose son is a student there and who is known to be very hard to please as far as he is concerned. Good news.

Friday morning to school for follow-up meeting about G's future and the college. Attended by ourselves (more time off work for Neil), headmistress of present school, teacher, welfare assistant, social worker, head of the college and careers officer. Eight of us and all for Gabriel.

Everyone is quite optimistic. The careers officer and social worker will look into funding – a vital component, almost the most vital, especially as there is talk of Gabriel possibly needing an extra member of staff, as he is provided with at the moment. The new Head will liaise with the school and visit to assess the new student and he will go there accompanied by one of his teachers for a few trial sessions. We're keeping our fingers very firmly crossed.

Saturday 5 February

Gabriel blew a fuse, as we say, on the way to the town this morning. He tried to pick some flowers from a garden and flew into one of his moods when stopped. He started to hit his head and scream so any idea of socialisation in the form of shopping had to be abandoned. I continued alone (lucky me) while Neil had to strong-arm him home – I certainly wouldn't have been able to manage him. Didn't want any lunch – always a bad sign – and continued to be confrontational (challenging) the rest of the day. Neil took him for a walk in the afternoon and he purposely walked on someone's garden and had to be dragged away. Later I had a tussle with him over music when I decided I'd had enough of it after five hours and switched off the hi-fi.

A little quieter in the evening which he spent wandering around with his shoes on the wrong feet and his coat on upside down. Gabriel is very attached to his coat, loves to wear it indoors and frequently wears it inside out or upside down – or both. Ate at least six oranges, his latest passion, including a Seville orange I'd bought for making marmalade. He's a boy and a half, as our neighbour once said.

Sunday 6 February

Gabriel gave us a break this morning spending most of it in his room lying on his bed fiddling. Aaaahhh. However, being autistic, his mood was quite different later in the day and he was manic all afternoon, pacing back and forth in the garden like a caged animal. Perhaps that is how he experiences himself. Caged.

When he is like this his vibrations, for want of a better word, are very disturbing. There is a tension in the air and meltdown, as Neil calls it, appears imminent – meltdown meaning a sudden bursting forth of anger and frustration in the form of screaming and head-banging. When he was younger the moods seemed to swing much more frequently, but even now, no matter how happy and calm he appears, there is no guarantee that his mood will last longer than the next minute – though the same can be said for the bad times too. It is this very instability that is so difficult to live with. A constant walking on eggshells.

3

'Sweet are the uses of adversity', or every stick has two ends

Never mind. Only tonight and Monday to go, only two more days, and then he's off to The Haven for three nights. Wonderful! Three nights respite, three days to relax, to do all – well, some – of the things we can't do when HE'S at home. And no need to do all the things we have to do when he's here. We can be a normal family.

It is a simple fact that a family with a handicapped child is in a sense a handicapped family, and I can't stress too much the importance of respite care for people in our situation. People like Gabriel or, say, a person suffering from Alzheimer's disease, or perhaps someone severely physically disabled, need watching over and attending to 24 hours a day, every day. If those who look after them are not to be ground down by the demands made on them they must have some relief, some respite. All carers need a break. Respite care gives us a breathing space, gives us a chance to recharge our batteries and to have some time for ourselves and our other children.

As must have become clear by now, our lives are severely circumscribed by Gabriel. We cannot enjoy together many of the activities that are taken for granted in most families. Simple things like visits to friends or places of interest. Going to a football match or shopping, to the cinema or a restaurant – all very difficult if not impossible with Gabriel. Family occasions, weddings, parties, school plays, speech days and sports days – again impossible with the Wild Boy. Most of these activities appear to have little or no meaning for him and perhaps for that reason, and also because of a dislike of crowds, they often prompt horrendous behaviour.

Of course when he was younger we attempted to do these things together – only to have to abandon them midway. Eventually we abandoned them almost completely and from then on Neil and I took turns accompanying our other boys while one of us stayed at home with Gabriel. The only outings he really enjoys are walks (and fortunately for us we enjoy walking), car drives (but he doesn't like to stop) and occasional visits to tolerant relatives.

Equally there are many 'at home' activities that are difficult to pursue with Gabriel around. Neil is interested in photography, but he could not contemplate setting up lights or getting out the chemicals for developing and printing when Gabriel is at home. Never mind about the problem of keeping him out of the darkroom. Or what about having friends round for a meal? Again difficult. He's almost certain to snatch food off their plates for a start (a habit everyone who has had anything to do with him has tried, and failed, to control). While we are busy enjoying their company he could be busy getting up to mischief elsewhere in the house. He might have a tantrum or a fit, or escape out of the front door in an unguarded moment. He might also do none of these things – though that is unlikely. The point is that we could never rely on him not to.

Happily all these pleasures are possible with respite care and we usually make the most of it. In fact as we can only enjoy them when Gabriel is away we value them all the more and I'm sure we get much more enjoyment on these occasions than people who can enjoy them at any time. Every stick has two ends.

Respite care is allocated according to need and circumstances: families with the most difficult children getting more than those with 'easier' children; single parent families getting more than families with two parents. At least this is the theory; it must be very difficult in practice to be fair. Sometimes there are simply not the facilities for those who need it most, such as the multiply handicapped who need full nursing care. Many of us parents have to fight our corner over these matters and have to accept that often those who shout loudest get the best service.

At any rate we are fortunate in having an adequate allocation allowing us to have a short break of a day or two every two to three weeks – we prefer to have little and often rather than longer breaks further apart. More rarely we have a whole week or even two, which is more difficult to arrange – but not impossible as long as one can be flexible. Finally, apart from respite The Haven is also there for cases of emergency.

Gabriel's respite (and don't forget he probably enjoys a change of scenery and a break from us – it's not all one way) is at a home founded and run by a local Mencap society. Here the kind and hard-working staff care for about half a dozen children including some with challenging behaviour. It is a large house in spacious grounds which allows Gabriel plenty of room to work off his energy, which he must enjoy after the confined space of our small house and garden. He has been going there regularly since he was 4 and is (nearly) always happy to go. If the respite falls during school time, as this week, his taxi and escort continue to transport him to and from school, returning him in the evening to The Haven instead of home.

Our respite is allocated a year in advance. We are asked if there are any dates we particularly want (for holidays, etc.) and those in charge do their best to please everyone, but naturally there is more demand at certain times of the year or for weekends and we must all take our turn. Otherwise, if there is an event we want to attend together we can only do so when Gabriel is away, so we are always pleased when something we wish to go to happens to fall on a respite day.

Perhaps one might ask at this stage what about babysitters? This was occasionally possible years ago when Gabriel was smaller and more manageable and for a while we had a treasure of a babysitter. But who could we find now to look after an obstreperous, hyper-active, unstable and challenging 15-year-old? What if he had a fit or a tantrum, or escaped? Who could we ask to change his nappies and wash his bottom? Such babysitters are few and far between – and of course have to be, deserve to be, well paid. No, better to leave him with the professionals. Let them have the responsibility and do the jumping up and down for the next three days. Meanwhile we can forget all about him, relax, leave the doors unlocked, eat our meals in peace and sleep in our own beds. And although we all like to go places when Gabriel is away, it is also lovely just to be at home with time to pursue our interests without having to be constantly on the alert. We can even appreciate such simple pleasures as putting our feet up for the evening and doing absolutely nothing!

I am not exaggerating when I say it might not have been possible to keep Gabriel living at home for so long had we not had adequate respite and I sincerely salute all the carers who, willingly or un-willingly, have managed without it.

Friday 11 February

When Gabriel is away we do our best to have nothing to do with autism and where possible avoid any functions or meetings con-nected with the world of mental handicap. We don't talk about him either – there is plenty of time for that when he is home. These little breaks are like holidays for us and leaving cares and preoccupations on one side is what a holiday is for. It's different for Jacob though, our 11-year-old.

'When's Gabriel coming home?' he asked this morning.

'Why d'you want to know?'

'It's boring without him.'!

I'm sure we'd all agree that life is never boring when Son Number Two is around but I for one certainly don't pine for him when he's away; yet having enjoyed a couple of free days I wasn't sorry to see our Madcap back this afternoon. He seemed pleased to be home – or did he? It's hard to tell really, he appears so indifferent to us most of the time. Actually he came home and carried on exactly as usual – rushed past me without looking, straight to his cupboard to find a twirler before tearing into the garden and running up and down until 6 o'clock.

Unfortunately he doesn't like the back door to be shut when he's outside and it was rather cold – but at least it was easier to check that he wasn't getting up to mischief. 'Mischief' here mostly consists in getting out of the garden, either by climbing over the gate into the street or over the fence into the neighbours' gardens. (Putting up a gate and new fences was the very first job to be done when we moved to this house, Gabriel being 4 at the time. Since then both gate and

Always on the move

fences have been altered to make them higher. Intricate trellises have also been built, all in an effort to contain him but none positively effective against an agile and determined 15-year-old.)

I used the word 'mischief' because that seems to be what is behind Gabriel's little escapades over the boundary. Part of the attraction is to 'wind us up', to provoke a reaction. Someone will have to run after him, shout at him, catch him and bring him back. Someone will have to engage with him in other words. He does it for that clichéd reason – to get attention. He shows his satisfaction when he has achieved it by grinning hugely, chuckling to himself or even laughing out loud. I think he also does it as he sees no reason why he should not explore wherever he likes even if he 'knows' by now that it is not allowed. Of course that fact too makes it attractive – the forbidden is always alluring, especially to a teenager, and one mustn't lose sight of the fact that beneath his autism Gabriel has plenty of characteristics in common with his normal peers.

Today however this teenager was content to stay in the garden and while I kept an eye on him I read his home/school book. His teacher reported that he had had a lively week and 'certainly kept us on our toes'. She asked us to cut his nails as staff had suffered a few scratches from him lately (they are not allowed to cut them without our permission). It also seems he is making progress in geography! The school timetable is linked to the National Curriculum (this consists for the majority of 'working towards Level 1') and covers the usual subjects with the objectives adapted to the pupil's abilities. Thus the aims in science for Gabriel are:

1.   To tolerate and enjoy a massage on his hands and feet.

2.   To learn to differentiate between litter and non-litter.

(!) An aim in English is: To develop an understanding of verbs related to his own activities using photographs. Etcetera. To go back to geography, the teacher's objective is to teach Gabriel to find his own way to the dustbins with a sack of refuse (presumably the result of the science period, objective 2). It seems that today he accomplished this task unaccompanied. This is progress – keep it up Gabes.

In the evening I encouraged him to dry himself after his bath, but he simply can't be bothered. He has the attention span of a moth and can't stop fiddling with his ribbon long enough to dry more than his face. Finally he put the towel over his head and carried on fiddling with the ribbon underneath it. Not a lot of progress there.

Saturday 12 February

A difficult day – Gabriel was in a stroppy mood. We went shopping as usual this morning but didn't dare take him into the baker's as there was a queue. Neil tried waiting with him outside but he came bursting in anyway and starting pushing and trying to grab and little children stood wide eyed and open mouthed at the sight of this Very

Naughty Boy. We only just managed to get home without incident as he was getting more and more wound up.

Refused to take his coat off for lunch. Gabriel invariably opposes every request and sometimes we have to ask a dozen times – he can't bear to obey first time. Today when asked to remove his coat he instantly decided not to and totally ignored us, defiantly sitting at the table with it on until Neil was forced to get tough. Thumping his chest in anger he bolted down his lunch in three minutes and rushed outside.

It was quite a pleasant afternoon, warm and sunny, so I busied myself in the garden while watching The One Possessed, who was pacing up and down as if driven by some uncontrollable force – as no doubt he was – and following the same route all afternoon until he had worn a muddy path across the lawn. Once when my back was turned he climbed over the fence into the neighbours', knocking over a couple of pots as he did so. Luckily they were out and the pots didn't break so I crept surreptitiously into their garden and straightened up a few bent leaves he had landed on and hoped they wouldn't notice anything.

Neil, Christian and Jacob went out for the evening leaving me on my own with our wild boy, who was still rushing about determinedly. He was determined first to get into the spare room which I had locked – probably because I'd locked it. He tried every key he could find and a few things besides – like teaspoons and tin-openers – until by chance he found the hidden key and got in. I decided not to confront him as I had the feeling he would win any battles this evening and by then a friend had come by with a bottle of wine to keep me company.

'How's Gabriel?' she asks, always an initial inquiry, 'Stable?'

'Not really,' I reply, 'He just has to be contrary. You say black and he says white – or would if he could talk.'

'But that's adolescence!' she exclaims and reluctantly I have to agree and wonder how long adolescence lasts in autism. At that moment the adolescent charges in, picks up the the wine and, eyeing me challengingly, very obstreperously and with great gusto, takes a few large swigs. (I didn't demur, just wished he'd have a bit more – it might quieten him down.) Then back upstairs with his coat on and up into the cupboard on top of the wardrobe, throwing out all the contents as he climbs in. Friend remarks that he's just like a monkey.

Gabriel likes a cupboard. Perhaps it's like a lair or a burrow to him, a place to hide, safe away from us all. I am reminded of a time years ago when we combed the neighbourhood for him thinking he had escaped, only to discover him at last and quite by chance sitting at the back of the airing cupboard. Anyway it was an evening dominated by cupboards for after a spell in the wardrobe he decided to try to get into another one. This one is kept padlocked as it contains photographic materials and chemicals and the first we knew about it was when he rushed downstairs and found a screwdriver. Gabriel can't actually use a screwdriver, but knows it's a TOOL and that a tool is necessary to open the door. The next two hours were spent trying to prise off the lock. (Plenty of attention there!) As he didn't succeed with the screwdriver he kept rushing downstairs for other 'tools', anything that might do the trick. But tonight he was defeated and the others had a good laugh later when they saw the assortment he'd used in the attempt: lying next to the screwdriver were several spoons now bent and useless, the bottle opener, the garlic press and the poker.

Sunday 13 February

Well of course I should have qualified it when I said that Gabriel had an extremely short attention span. The truth is that, like everyone else, his attention span is short for things that are of no interest to him – such tasks as learning to put his shoes on the right feet or brushing his teeth – but when it comes to solving a problem such as a locked cupboard, with who knows what inside, his persistence knows no bounds. Thus this morning as soon as he was up he forgot about breakfast and made straight for the padlock, finally managing to get the whole contraption off the door. Not a bad effort considering his main instrument was the bread knife and that it was a particularly heavy lock put on to replace a smaller one he'd levered off a few weeks previously.

Another common characteristic – never take the easy way, and even if the door is open, climb through the window

Gabriel's skill in this respect pales however in comparison with a friend's son. He was to spend a few days in Great Ormond Street Hospital and before leaving him there his mother warned staff that he shouldn't be left alone for long with any sort of tool as he was liable to use it on the fixtures and fittings. Sure enough later that day a nurse returned to his room to find he had unscrewed some skirting and removed a floor board with the aid of a *teaspoon*. He was just 5 years old. (But why should he want to do such a thing? Because it was there? To discover what was underneath?) Obviously the answer for us was not an even bigger padlock, so I removed the contents and hid them away elsewhere.

Having achieved his object Gabriel then lost interest and passed the rest of the day as usual, that is either running about fiddling or lying about fiddling – which he has done day in day out more or less all his life. Nowadays, thank goodness, more time is spent lying, whereas when he was younger he only ran; but either way he fiddles and twirls.

This he does with great absorption, watching fascinatedly as his laces and strings spin and turn. From time to time he stops, puts one down and selects another from his Collection (collections of one kind or another are often very important to autistic people), then continues whirling them round again and again. Now he dips them in water; round and round they go as he watches the droplets sparkle and fly off – all over the windows, dammit. The laces become knotted together and he comes to one of us to untangle them – there is a fleeting regard, a brief moment of contact, then off he goes again. Up and down and round and round. Now he has a little rest, either sitting cross-legged by his cupboard (the one where he sleeps) or lying on his stomach on the floor, but all the time twirling, twirling. Although Gabriel has no coherent speech he uses his voice continuously to accompany himself with faint murmurings, squeaks, cries, grunts and occasional chortles or a little contented humming.

'Well, he seems happy enough,' people say watching him, a slightly bemused expression on their faces. So indeed he appears a great deal of the time. Though we know that the possibility of an outburst is never far below the surface and he might suddenly start to shriek or slap himself, these episodes are usually short-lived and as he gets older they become rarer.

Monday 14 February

Although as I have said Gabriel's outbursts are not too frequent, they can still be quite violent and can present difficulties at school. Sometimes for the sake of others or for his own safety or to avoid damage to property he needs to be controlled and restrained. How he is controlled on these occasions is set out in a 'Behavioural Programme involving the Denial of a Child's Rights'. In other words every pupil has a right not to be held, removed to a quiet room or restrained in any way. However, in certain circumstances staff feel that these are the only ways to manage some children – Gabriel of course being one. Parents are consulted and asked to suggest and approve programmes and a review of the programme is carried out every six months.

So, to school today for a review of Gabriel's Denial of Rights Programme. The meeting is conducted by the school psychiatrist and attended by the principal, G's teacher and myself. The behaviours that cause concern are: escape attempts, self-injurious behaviour such as pinching himself and headbanging, pinching and scratching others, pulling displays off walls, grabbing food at mealtimes, and sitting down and refusing to move (passive resistance).

We go through the list and nothing too drastic is recommended. We all agree that when he makes a run for it, it is better to grab him by his clothing rather than by his hands or arms, which only exacerbates matters. On other occasions – when headbanging or when he refuses to move – it is necessary for two members of staff to 'escort him using an underarm lift – the Backward Loddon Lift'. When he pinches others on minibus journeys they find the best way to contain his aggressive behaviour is to tie the ends of his jumper sleeves! Temper tantrums are dealt with by either letting him loose in the playground or leaving him in a quiet place. And so on. All occasions when it has been necessary to carry out any of these strategies are entered in the School Sanctions Records and there had been 17 such incidents since the previous review.

I feel this is all quite fair and justified knowing the difficulties he presents and I am only too thankful that they continue to put up with him, being aware that he is one of their most challenging pupils. Yet not only do they put up with him but they go to great lengths on his and our behalf – he arrived home this afternoon with a Valentine's card for me! Lots of crumpled pink tissue stuck on in the shape of a heart and kisses inside (well, scribble actually) from Gabriel. And I never knew he cared.

Later I had to keep him locked indoors as some water pipes in the garden were being repaired and it would have impossible for the workmen to do their job with him in and out of their muddy trench. He spent an hour trying to get out. It seemed unfair and must be frustrating, but oh if only he understood more.

Tuesday 15 February

Came home from school today in completely different clothes from the ones he'd set out in. They were not his own but out of a store of cast-offs kept at school and he looked a real orphan in the ill-fitting assortment – trousers that were too short and a horrible garish sweatshirt that he had put on back to front. Luminous pink socks were the finishing touch. Not that he minds of course. Raising his eyebrows, escort Tom handed over a plastic sack containing his own dripping clothes – coat included. The explanation: Gabriel loves swimming and having got dressed after today's swim suddenly decided (and not for the first time) he wanted more and had therefore jumped back in the pool fully clothed.

I can imagine how pleased the staff were and I'm sure they probably had quite a job getting him out again. I could just picture it – Gabriel ignoring all their requests to get out and, smiling to himself at their consternation, carefully keeping just out of reach. He'd probably kept that up for at least ten minutes before finally condescending to do as they asked. Exasperating is his middle name.

Perhaps because he'd had his fun at school today he was amenable and calm when he got home and spent a relaxing evening with his twirlers. I should say that Gabriel, even when he is in a good mood, very rarely sits with us. He is a loner, as they say, and even if he sits in the same room as the rest of the family he will invariably sit in a corner with his back to us, only coming to us for his wants or needs. Although I feel sure he would rather be with us than anywhere else, he rarely shows spontaneous affection towards any of us. He gives and accepts no hugs, no cuddles, no kisses, but only bestows an engaging smile on his favourites from time to time or very occasionally sits for a moment on someone's lap; if we try to hold him he struggles to free himself.

Age 13 in Dorset where he spent most of the time fully dressed in the river at the bottom of my mother's garden. Here looking challenging – 'Come and get me if you can'

This aloofness is typical of most autistic people and understandably a characteristic that many parents find especially difficult to cope with – to have so little response when one has suffered so much on their account is sometimes very hard. I quote one mother: 'For me, one of the most difficult aspects of Alan's autism has been his failure to recognise me and his lack of warmth.' When Alan was 4 he had to go back to hospital after a weekend at home. He suddenly started to cry and jumped on to his mother's lap saying 'no, no, no' and, as she wrote 'It was the only time he's ever behaved as if I was his mother.' Another woman wrote that her daughter had turned and hugged her for the first time at the age of 36 – and that the reason why was a complete mystery.

People often have a sentimental view of the mentally handi-capped as being 'very loving', as they often put it, but although that may be true of many it is certainly not always the case. On the other hand showing none of the usual signs of affection need not mean it isn't there or cannot grow. We need to recognise that the aloofness is part of them and their way of being human. Donna Williams is autistic and has written several books about her experiences. She also hated to be held and explains: 'Responding with an indirect or detached manner is not synonymous with indifference.'

As all was quiet on the Gabriel front we spent a couple of hours that evening drafting a letter to the school which had turned him down; not because of the refusal but because of the way the application had been handled. It should have been written weeks ago but we seem to have endless paperwork and form-filling to do on Gabriel's behalf and sometimes just can't find the energy for it.

Thursday 17 February

Escort Tom said he'd 'been a naughty boy again' at school but didn't elaborate. He spent the evening in what I call rummage mode and Neil calls exploring. This consists of turning out cupboards and drawers. He turfs everything out onto the floor, appearing very intent on looking for something, and dashes from room to room as if recalling another place this elusive 'something' might be. The house begins to look as if we've been burgled and I make an effort to ignore the chaos of drawers spilling over and heaps of belongings lying on the floor – no point in picking things up yet. I also make an effort to ignore the feeling of tension that is emanating from Gabriel, like high voltage electricity crackling from a pylon. What is he looking for?

Often these tense moods presage a late night and a fit, but to our surprise and relief he took himself off to bed quite early, firmly closing the door behind him. He'd had enough of us and himself.

Friday 18 February

Gabriel must have had a fit as we'd half expected because he was impossible to rouse this morning. I knew he probably wouldn't wake until late afternoon so there was no question of sending him to school – nor any question of me leaving the house today.

In the afternoon when he woke he started masturbating (or humping the sofa) and I had to send him to his room. Can't really let him do that sort of thing in the sitting room. Otherwise quiet and an early night. For me too – next week is half-term and I'll need all the energy I can muster.

4

More life and times on Planet Autism

Monday 21 February

Half-term all week.

Although the purpose of school is to educate, however widely one may interpret that, for us the main advantage is that Gabriel is looked after each day. It is true he has made, and continues to make, some progress – in geography, for example – but it is difficult to be optimistic about what he can be taught when he is still so utterly helpless as regards his own needs after twelve years of schooling. Being realistic, it appears that Gabriel is ineducable (if that word is to have any meaning) so that we no longer have any great expectations of school and are simply glad he has somewhere to go each day. He is out of the house for eight hours and during that time someone else is responsible for him, wiping his bottom, picking up the shredded leaves and making sure he doesn't disappear over the fence – and if he learns something useful that is an added bonus.

We also need the time to do all the necessary chores and errands that can't be done with him around. Things like shopping. Though we take Gabriel down the town at the weekend this is more to give him an outing and a lesson in socialisation than really to shop; I have not done the shopping alone with him for a long time. Activities such as decorating are equally impossible with him around – all that wet paint, and so on. Even cooking used to be stressful with his continual interference and grabbing at hot pans, and I often prepared the evening meal as far as possible before he came home.

Half-term and no school for a week. I recall how in the past I used to dread all school holidays. What long days they were and how slowly they seemed to pass as I ticked them off to the next schoolday or time in respite. What had other mothers to complain about (as they frequently did) compared with looking after the Wild Boy? Six normal children would be easier any day. In fact on one memorable occasion my sister and I actually took six assorted cousins, including Gabriel to the beach and we took hour-long turns – one to watch the autistic cousin, one to watch the other five, the latter being by far the easier option.

I dreaded the holidays for two reasons: first because of the demands Gabriel made on my stamina and patience; second because of the feeling that I was neglecting the other children. This is why respite is so important.

The holidays are still hard work but I've learned to pace myself now and I no longer need to worry myself about the other two. Christian is away studying and Jacob is old enough and independent enough to look after himself most of the time. He's had to be. Nowadays my main problem is controlling Gabriel as he gets bigger – he is taller than me now – and more obstreperous. I have almost given up taking him out as he is too strong and unpredictable. He can suddenly fly into a fury because he wants to go left when I want to go right and as he has no sense of danger and no traffic sense and can run faster than me it is too much of a risk and too nerve-racking.

In fact I've lost my nerve after a recent incident. I asked Gabriel if he wanted to go for a walk and it was clear he liked the idea by the speed with which he found his coat. We set off, I thought, to go over the fields at the back of the house, a walk with no traffic and no shops. Gabriel however had a different idea and immediately started sprinting in the direction of the town, ignoring all my requests to come back. The first shop he went into – I couldn't stop him – was the newsagents where he helped himself to a packet of sweets and a carton of juice. Calling hurriedly to the shopkeeper that I would return later to pay for them as I had no money with me I followed him out as he ripped open the sweets and spilled them on the pavement. He wouldn't let me pick them up or help him with the carton, which he'd also ripped open then tucked under his arm while he bent down to pick up the sweets, naturally squeezing the juice out as he did so. With orange juice dripping down his clothes he gathered them up and stuffed all of them in his mouth at once, grit and dust included. Then he pushed me out of the way and strode on down the high street, crossing roads without looking, as I ineffectually tried to head him off in another direction. Passing a bakery (not our regular one) he noticed some jam tarts. They were behind a glass counter, but that didn't deter Gabriel who immediately barged in and climbed onto the counter to reach the tarts and help himself. I pulled his coat, asking him, telling him, *pleading* with him to get down and trying to explain the situation to the assistant. I didn't dare pull too hard for fear of making him all the more determined, while an awful vision of the entire counter collapsing in a shower of broken glass, squashed cakes, cream and blood filled my imagination. The assistant – a young girl, probably imagining the same – was backing away in alarm as this apparently crazy 15-year-old boy tried to climb over the counter. I begged her to give him a tart, even though I had no money, before a quick-thinking customer offered to pay. Gabriel was given two tarts, disaster was averted – and I was left a nervous wreck. Like many people with learning difficulties he is extremely strong-willed. At the same time he has no social inhibitions, nor comprehension – at least I don't think he has, though I can't help feeling sometimes he does know what he is doing and it pleases him to create a little mayhem.

As Neil is self-employed and is a very conscientious father he usually contrives to be around as much as possible during the holidays in order to help with Gabriel. Not today though, so we are confined to house and garden while Jacob is constantly in and out with his friends and I have to remind them to make sure the gate is shut and the front door locked. They are only young; naturally they forget and I swear Gabriel can smell an open door, so I have to keep checking.

As usual he starts the day fairly calmly. He takes a long time to get going and it is well into the morning before he is up, washed, dressed and breakfasted. He disappears upstairs to the landing to unravel a bit more of the carpet there which he has been unravelling over a period of about two years – he's undone about half of it now. The threads make good twirlers and he has bundles of the carpet threads in his cupboard. We call him the Gerbil when he is in a shredding and unravelling mood as the mound of shredded paper and wool gets bigger and bigger resembling a (giant) gerbil's nest. This keeps him happy for an hour or more while I potter in the kitchen. Suddenly I hear a shriek. I gather myself together. Then another. He thuds down the stairs screaming and hitting his head and I dodge as he races by.

'What's the matter with him?' asks one of Jacob's friends, who hasn't visited here before and is looking nervous.

'Nothing, it's just one of his moods,' Jacob replies off-handedly. 'Let's go out.'

Gabriel gets more and more furious, pinching his forehead and the back of his neck and letting out bellows of rage as he charges back and forth. He catches sight of a small rolling pin, picks it up and hits his head with it. I try to stay calm and quietly remove a saucepan of hot food from the stove, remembering an occasion not so long ago when in a similar mood he dashed a full pan of hot soup to the floor and over his feet, burning them quite badly. I tell him firmly to go to his room and scream up there – sometimes he obeys but today he ignores me. There's nothing for it but to ride out the storm and after half an hour the storm blows itself out without incident. He can't help it; he's a victim of his moods like anyone else, but is less able to control himself. Plenty of ballast in the form of a large dish of chicken noodles reinforces a calmer happier mood and he returns to his unravelling.

Tomorrow he's off to The Haven for two nights respite and when I collect him on Thursday the week will be almost over.

Thursday 24 February

Collected the lad at midday. Had been 'in a lovely mood' – thank goodness. No problems. Back home it had snowed and he enjoyed being in the garden, wandering about kicking it and picking it up and examining it. He was soon soaked but that didn't stop him sitting down in it – he didn't seem to notice the cold or wet although one would think it instinctual not to sit in a cold wet place. Even Gabriel's instincts don't seem to function normally, in fact we've noticed lately that he doesn't always realise when he's hungry, getting very upset yet not asking for food. (Donna Williams writes that she also had difficulty in recognising when she was hungry and had to remind herself to eat: 'I tried to remember to eat but had no understanding of my own sense of hunger.')

Later Gabriel was in a very provocative vein. (He's 'just a wind-up merchant' according to some.) He kept trying to take an important piece of paper from Christian, who is home for a few days, and when he eventually succeeded he tore it in half and then, as Christian tried to retrieve it, tore it up smaller and ate it. Later he attempted several times (fifteen or twenty) to take away the book I was reading and finally tore out a couple of pages. I was so incensed I screamed at him full pitch and hurt my throat. (I know, I know, he's only been back a few hours, but he gets to you like that.) Neil gave him a strict telling off but was finding it difficult not to laugh at the sight of him pressing himself into a corner, hoping to disappear into the wall and at the same time looking into the middle distance and blinking rapidly. All to signify 'it was nothing to do with me, I don't know what you're talking about, I just wanted attention. Anyway if I don't look at you I can't hear you and you can't see me…' and expressed with blinks and grunts and a lot of chest thumping before he disappeared upstairs.

Does he understand anything?

Half an hour later he appeared in the living room naked and with a dirty bottom. He had stripped off in his room, including dirty pants. There was shit on the duvet, shit on the carpet and shit on the stairs. Yes, he's back.

Friday 25 February

Fit. I spent most of the day trying to keep him awake so he would sleep tonight but constant prodding, exhorting or literally pulling Gabriel to his feet is almost harder work than looking after him when he is awake. I decided to at least take advantage of his sleepiness and to cut his hair.

Haircuts have always been a problem as he is unable to sit still for more than a few seconds and resents being touched or interfered with. (We have tried the barber and I'm not sure who the experience was most stressful for – Gabriel, the barber or ourselves.) He is also very possessive of cut hair or nail parings and tries to put them back and once even found and reinserted some snot I had surreptitiously removed from his nose! Being tired after a fit he is more amenable – doesn't get up and run away quite so often leaving a trail of cut hair – and I can usually do a reasonable job, cutting it as short as possible so it lasts. Today it was a tiny bit tricky doing the back as he insisted on keeping his coat on and the hood got in the way but even so the end result was a vast improvement. He looks so wild when it gets long.

In the evening Neil telephoned the organiser of the Club to say we would not be sending Gabriel again. The Club is very commend-ably run by staff and boys at the local public school in the name of service to the community. Once a week the mentally disabled children who live in the town are collected and taken to the school where they play in the gym with the boys. Most of them thoroughly enjoy it and their parents are grateful for the trouble the boys and staff go to, but Gabriel has never been keen to go in spite of our encouragement. The last time he went he ran amok and Neil was summoned to bring him home.

He does not conform to the cosy picture many people have of those with learning disabilities – that of lovable, affectionate simple-tons – and when he screams or hits himself they start to wonder what is wrong, if he is ill or has a pain or is hungry. What is wrong of course is that he is *autistic* and that's how he is – sometimes very unhappy and liable to sudden mood swings and erratic behaviour.

The organiser, who had once told us how well she got on with Gabriel and thought they had a 'special understanding', sounded relieved at the news – and who could blame her?

Saturday 26 February

Hyper hyper active all day. Did not stop. Neil worked in the garden and kept G. out there with him (to give me a break). We thought it better not to attempt shopping with him so I went alone, glad to get away. Met Mary with her son Geoffrey, who is as much of a handful as Gabriel, though different and a few years younger. He tends to bite and I am full of admiration for her shopping with him on her own as he lunges and pulls at people.

We'd received info about a little playscheme at Easter and wondered whether to send our children. It only occupies four mornings of the holiday but that is enough to give us a short breathing space and time to do something with our other children, but we're not sure they can cope. Mary had seen three helpers struggling with Geoffrey last year and she felt bad about putting them to so much trouble; as for our boy, he had made one of his epic escapes. His attendant had taken him to the toilet for a wee and naturally enough had waited for him outside the door. When it seemed he was taking rather a long time she opened the door only to find he had vanished through the window. There was panic all round, sorting out the other children and organising a search party before, having been alerted by an observant lorry driver, he was found a considerable distance away on a busy main road. Mary and I decided to keep our sons at home as, although these schemes are set up to help us, we feel bad if our children are too troublesome and as if in some way we're to blame for their misdemeanours.

He didn't sleep all night. Carried on through Sunday too without a yawn. I was sure he'd drop eventually (I nearly did) but he managed to keep going till midnight – and that's another half-term over.

Monday 28 February

Back to school.

In the evening I went out with the local contact group – Mums only tonight – for our annual pub dinner. When we meet we don't ask after each other but always how our respective children are getting on and as usual we spent a lot of time complaining about the 'authorities' and the problems we have with them.

Ann's son, James, is almost 19 and about to leave school. She has found a day centre she likes and considers suitable for him and James has been offered a place – but who is going to pay for it? She and her husband are getting ready for the battle ahead as 'they' have told them their son can only be funded for two and a half days a week. But James has about ten fits a day (his fits are quite different from Gabriel's being shorter but very frequent). Ann has a bad back and cannot lift him when he falls and of course cannot take him out on her own for fear of a fit, which means she will be confined to the house with him. She already often has to keep her son at home because of his fits and migraines and her own health is not good. Her husband is considering looking for part-time work rather than full time in order to help more with their only child – but that is not easy either.

Christine's son Matthew is about 25 and has Down's syndrome. He is quite 'high functioning' – able to read and write a bit – and lives in a flat a few miles away with two other mentally handicapped adults. In theory this is a marvellous example of what Care in the Community can be. In practice though they are left to fend for themselves to a degree which far exceeds their capabilities. They live relatively independently – too much so – and the only back-up they receive is a five-minute visit from carers each morning and evening. In the morning they are given a daily allowance of their money. It is doled out each day to help them budget and to prevent them from blowing the week's money in one day. But can they really look after themselves, I ask? What about cleaning the flat? Can they operate the washing machine? What about a sensible diet? Christine is very worried. Matthew has arthritis and needs help getting in and out of the bath; he can't manage it in fact so doesn't bother. If she doesn't check he doesn't think of such details as cutting his toe-nails and so on. As he tends to spend most of his money at the chip shop down the road, he is getting enormously fat. As for the washing machine, he puts all his clothes in unsorted, then turns the dial until things start happening and that's it. Inevitably the clothes come out looking

worse than when they went in, even to the point of being un-
wearable. So much for Care in the Community.

Linda's daughter Emma is very severely handicapped both physically and mentally and has needed full nursing care all her life. Her
parents have had their house adapted to her needs and Linda has
provided the care – with very little respite as facilities for looking
after children as fragile as Emma are few and far between. Emma is
14 now and is getting very heavy for Linda to lift on her own. She
and her husband want a hoist. (The family receive some care in the
home as a form of respite when helpers come to them, but *they* are not
allowed to lift Emma without help.) The 'authorities' however are
unwilling to pay for a hoist – even though without it it will soon be
impossible to keep Emma at home and she will have to be taken into
care, a much more costly option and one her parents are not yet ready
for.

Janet's three children, all with Down's syndrome, have been
fostered by Janet and her husband since birth. She has recently been
widowed but wouldn't dream of not continuing to care for the
children, who are now teenagers and going through the difficult
throes of adolescence. And so it goes on.

I cannot help admiring all of them, but especially those who do
not have the support of a partner. As well as Janet, out of our group of
ten there are three women here tonight who are divorced and have
managed on their own for many years, with sleepless nights, restricted
social lives and full responsibilities for their very demanding offspring, yet remaining unswervingly loyal to them. One meets many
unsung heroines (and occasionally heroes) in this situation. But we
haven't come to spend the evening talking about our children or
complaining about the school bus or the new speech therapist; we
have come to enjoy ourselves in the company of good friends. The
other customers in the bar are not to know that we have been drawn
together by circumstance rather than choice and are unaware of how
our common plight not only binds us but deepens our understanding
and feelings for one another. To them we are just a group of mostly
middle-aged women out for a 'hen party' – as indeed we are.

Wednesday 2 March

Fit – so another 'non' day.

Gabriel's fits are becoming more of a problem. Too often we are having days like these when he cannot go to school because of the drowsiness following a fit; and too often the sleepy days are followed by wide-awake nights when neither he nor we can sleep.

Although Gabriel suffered from epileptic fits as an infant he was totally free of seizures for more than nine years – until they started again at the age of 12, when we naturally recommenced the homoeopathic remedy he had had as an infant. This time however the treatment had no effect and the fits continued to be as frequent as ever. Knowing that it would be extremely stressful to take him to a hospital for the various necessary tests – a fact not always appreciated by doctors and nurses – we asked for a consultation at a specialised paediatric unit situated in the grounds adjoining his school. This was where Gabriel was assessed before being admitted to the school and the medical staff there have very close links with the school and can see the children in the classroom if necessary. Permission for this was refused and it took several letters and phone calls (and weeks) before our request was granted.

The paediatrician there knew of our reluctance to embark on a course of anti-epileptic drugs and suggested one final option. According to her, sometimes fits can be caused because of a deficiency in certain trace elements and she therefore arranged for him to be tested. This entailed going to a clinic in London where they would stick a small plaster (a sweat patch) on Gabriel's back, removing it an hour later for analysis. We were not surprised though when Gabriel removed it instantly – he has never tolerated plasters or bandages, even when badly cut or hurt in some way – and after three attempts we had to give up. A blood sample would of course have shown any deficiencies he might have but we could see him tolerating that even less. Since neither blood nor sweat were available a hair sample had to be used as an alternative, which, after analysis indicated that Gabriel was in fact lacking in various trace elements which were duly prescribed him.

A month has now passed since he started taking the tablets but so far they appear to have had no effect and we are coming under increasing pressure to 'forget all these hare-brained ideas' and to settle for more orthodox treatment. Undeniably we are reaching the point where the adverse effects of the fits outweigh any potentially adverse effects of the drugs. We'll just give it a little longer.

Friday 3 March

All correspondence today was connected with Gabriel. To our fury and disgust one of the allowances he receives had come up for renewal and had been awarded at a lower rate. The allowance consists of two components – care and mobility – and until now Gabriel has had the higher rate for both. (The mobility component, or help with getting around, has only recently been awarded to people like Gabriel. Previously, one literally had to have difficulty moving – trouble with feet, legs, etc. – and behavioural difficulties were not considered a valid reason. Fortunately it is now recognised that disruptive behaviour in the street or on public transport, a lack of road sense or sense of danger and a need to be accompanied all make moving around as difficult as a physical disability.) We will definitely contest this decision as our circumstances have not changed. If anything they are more difficult than when we applied two years ago so there should be no reason for a change. No reason was given either, we were just informed that from now on he would receive less. Bloody cheek. One does get fed up having to contest decisions and fight for every right. It's true we're used to it by now and know the ropes – still, it's been a steep learning curve since Son Number Two came into our lives nearly sixteen years ago.

5

'When did you know?'

Gabriel was born on Tuesday 25 April 1978. It was a cold but sunny spring day and I woke early, aware of a vaguely familiar sensation in my womb. Nudging Neil awake I whispered, 'Baby's coming, we'd better get up.'

We were living in Denmark then, about thirty miles from Copenhagen, which was where the baby was to be born. I had to pack my bag and we also had to take Christian, then aged 4, to friends before setting off.

It was with some trepidation that I got into the car for, although I had been looking forward to it, Christian's birth had been a little rough. This time however everything went according to the book; there were no problems and at midday after a very easy, and yes, enjoyable labour, Gabriel slipped into the world.

His appearance was immediately striking: he had a huge shock of black hair which grew from low down his forehead and although he had not been due for another two weeks he was obviously ready judging by the length of it – it was even long enough to be combed with a parting after his first wash! We both remarked on the hair and his dark colouring but Neil was also particularly struck by what he could only describe as his 'wild and almost ancient' appearance, as he noted in a diary at the time. Though he put this down to the baby's shock of being thrust into the world, he has since always considered it significant.

Significant or not, Gabriel's appearance certainly distinguished him from the Danish babies who were all fair and totally bald. Anyway we agreed it gave him character and we were both delighted with our second son. Christian too had been looking forward to having a brother and playmate, especially as we were rather isolated in Denmark, and here he was at last – a lovely healthy boy.

Gabriel and I had to stay longer than planned in this excellent hospital as he was slightly jaundiced and was given several days of phototherapy. This meant him lying naked under lights, but I was assured it was a routine procedure and although it made it difficult to breastfeed my baby I insisted on continuing to do so. The only other fact of note was a strange cry that he let out from time to time – a piercing bird-like cry quite unlike the normal cry of a newborn baby. I remarked on it but didn't think anything of it. Nonetheless the doctors took him away and examined his throat. They could find nothing amiss however and after a few days he stopped making the strange noise. His face uncrumpled and we were ready to go home.

We passed the rest of the year in Denmark and Gabriel turned into a handsome and bonny baby. It is true, Neil once remarked, that he was not very generous with his smiles but he mostly seemed content. He ate and slept reasonably well. Like all babies he did his share of

A few months old in bed with Christian – looking off into the distance

crying but, as we remembered, was no more fretful than Christian had been or any other babies we came in contact with. He seemed perfectly normal.

In January when Gabriel was eight months old we moved back to England and I travelled ahead with the two boys. One night a few days after we had arrived I woke up to hear strange noises coming from the baby in the cot next to my bed. When I looked at him he appeared to be having some kind of fit. This was the first definite sign that all was not well.

This fit was followed a week or two later by another and then another, and so began the long association with doctors and hospitals. Soon it was arranged for Gabriel to go into hospital for tests and I was able to stay there with him. The tests revealed nothing; his ECG was normal, he didn't have a brain tumour and there was no discernible reason for the epilepsy. We left with a prescription to control the fits.

However Neil and I had always been interested in alternative medicine and were very reluctant to embark on this course before having explored other avenues. We searched for and found an orthodox doctor who was also trained in homoeopathy and was willing to prescribe a homoeopathic remedy for the epilepsy. In his opinion it was worth a try.

In the following year – from the age of twelve to eighteen months – it became more and more apparent to some that Gabriel was not developing normally. As soon as Neil's mother, who'd had four children herself and worked with babies and young children, heard about the fits she exclaimed 'I *knew* there was something wrong with that baby. I couldn't explain what, but...' My mother, who'd also had four of us, was worried that he wouldn't look at her; but we ourselves were unable to see the wood for the trees. Because his physical progress was normal, because he had sat up and walked when he should, because he looked the picture of health with his rosy cheeks and plump limbs, we ascribed everything else to his epilepsy – and by now he sometimes had several fits in a week. His fretfulness and apparent disorientation, the sudden and unaccountable screams and the disinclination to use language all seemed readily explained by the convulsions.

Some signs that all was not right were nebulous and only significant in retrospect. The fact that he never played with any of his toys but preferred to clutch an old talcum powder tin or jangle a plug and chain we thought unremarkable. After all, who didn't know of children who were happy with a string of cotton reels or a few saucepan lids? We even thought it rather cute, and it was years before we discovered that a lack of interest in toys or a tendency to play with them inappropriately was a typical feature of autism.

Then there was the time I pushed him up the hill to the farm near our home to see the cows. We stood at the gate only inches from their soft breathy bodies while they waited to be herded into the milking shed, but Gabriel not only appeared totally uninterested but almost seemed not to see them. I cast my mind back to Christian. He had always been fascinated by animals and on one occasion at about the same age – eighteen months – had been so excited by the ducks in the park that he had tipped head first into the pond. I began to wonder what could be wrong.

Another significant sign – in retrospect that is – was his hyperactivity. (Actually although my pregnancy had been completely trouble free and normal, Gabriel had been a particularly active baby in the womb, endlessly twisting, turning and kicking.) No sooner had he learned to walk than he ran – and ran – and ran. He was never still. But then, we said to each other, all toddlers are active and 'into everything' and again, for the time being, it didn't seem to us that he was different from any other child. Besides there was a lot in the news at the time about hyperactivity, connecting it with additives or particular foods. Maybe that was the problem.

Yet while the doubts continued to niggle and he still hadn't uttered a word friends sought to reassure us. 'I don't know what you're worrying about,' said one, a father of two children, after spending the weekend with us, 'He seems perfectly alright to me.' Others told us that Winston Churchill or some such great man hadn't spoken until he was nearly three. Or that so-and-so's brother or friend had had a lot of fits, still had the occasional fit in fact, and look

at him now. A professor at university. And so on. And of course we
longed with all our hearts to believe they were right.

But however much we longed suddenly to find we had imagined
all these worries, as Gabriel's third year began it became more and
more difficult to explain away his behaviour or excuse it with the
epilepsy. Above all was the fact that he still wasn't speaking, and since
he didn't speak people suggested he might be deaf. Perhaps it was
not a question of not speaking but of not hearing, especially as he
seemed to have no understanding of language, not even 'yes' and
'no', and didn't respond to his name. Not only that, but if an armful
of saucepans were dropped behind him he would not show the
slightest reaction. Perhaps even if he were not profoundly deaf his
hearing might be impaired in some way or to some degree.

A hearing test was duly attempted but it was very difficult,
impossible even to assess Gabriel's responses, and after it we were
none the wiser. In any case Neil and I never really doubted he could
hear (though we agreed his hearing might not be normal) as we had
seen him stand raptly by the hi-fi apparently listening to and deeply
absorbed by the music. We were not to know until years later that
many parents of autistic children have wondered if their children
were deaf or hearing impaired. In fact in a booklet put out by the
National Autistic Society there is a short résumé of the sort of worries
professionals often hear which begins: 'I can't quite put my finger on
it, but there's something wrong with John. At first we thought he was
deaf...'

Increasingly Gabriel seemed to be in a world of his own – a cliché,
but no other words described his state so accurately. His lack of
response to others was now becoming more marked for not only did
he not react to their words but he wouldn't look at them; his attention
always seemed to be focused on objects rather than people. There
was the favourite object of the moment, the talc tin or plug and chain
that would be turned round and scrutinised endlessly. At other times
he just gazed fascinatedly at his hands, twisting and turning them
before his eyes. The designs and textures of certain fabrics were
another source of interest and he would examine them closely or

scratch them to hear the noise they made or he would gaze into space seemingly engrossed in watching motes of dust in the sunlight.

Although some of these activities could be seen to have their attractions – who hasn't been bewitched by the luminous haze revealed in a sunbeam? – when they excluded any interest in people it began to get worrying. Why wouldn't he look us in the eyes? Or even look at us at all? (We didn't realise that he did observe people, but so quickly and surreptitiously that he only gave the appearance of not looking.) So totally did he ignore one acquaintance who was visiting and meeting him for the first time that she commented she now knew was it was like to be invisible.

The obsessiveness too – especially with twirlers – was consolidating from what had been a droll quirk to a dominating and all-encompassing activity. Plugs and chains and silk scarves were relentlessly pressed into service and soon vegetation followed. There is a photograph in the family album of Gabriel at this age in the garden sitting in the middle of a large clump of some low spreading plant and I remember that over several sunny days he uprooted every bit of it. He has been addicted to vegetation ever since; I can never resist referring to the obsession with plants as a hardy and perennial one.

Yet maddening though the twiddling was, what affected us most was the hyperactivity. Up until the age of about two, although the fits were deeply worrying, looking after Gabriel had not been that different from looking after any other infant. But by that age a normal 2-year-old is beginning to acquire some independence – in feeding, toiletting, dressing and so forth. Gabriel on the other hand was requiring more and more of our attention. When he was awake it seemed as if he never stopped moving. Looking through the family photographs of that period in every one he is either racing by in the background, twirlers flying, or struggling and squirming on someone's lap where he is being held still for the camera. He was like a whirlwind tearing through the house night and day.

Also once he could move freely it was not long before he started to wander and because he understood so little he had no sense of danger. One day when Gabriel was about 2 a white-faced and shaken

*Once he could walk he **ran** and was never still or without a twirler*

van driver came to the door with our son in his arms. We lived at that time in a country lane and I had left him playing in the garden when I had gone indoors to answer the telephone. He had left our garden, crossed the lane, found his way through a hedge and neighbour's garden and down a drive to a fairly busy road about 150 yards away. Here the shocked driver had narrowly missed hitting him as he sat in the middle of the road. From then on he could never be trusted out of sight and if we went out anywhere he had to be held or wear a harness in case he rushed heedlessly into danger.

All of this time we had not seen a doctor or paediatrician since the tests in hospital apart from the homoeopath who was treating Gabriel for the seizures. Maybe we both suffered from an overdose of hubris but, as we said to each other, what could they do? There was no magic pill which was going to make our son speak. Nevertheless the hyperactivity, the violent mood swings which were developing and his increasingly erratic and bizarre behaviour meant of course we had to see someone eventually.

We moved house again a few months before Gabriel's third birthday and decided to address these problems as soon as we were installed in our new home. In the meantime there had been one huge improvement – the fits had gradually become less frequent until they ceased altogether (and did not reappear for nine and a half years). Now his behaviour could no longer be put down to the epilepsy. We asked our GP to arrange an appointment for us with a paediatrician in Great Ormond Street.

Appointments were always a nightmare – especially if we had to wait, which invariably we did. Gabriel was all over the waiting room, running down corridors, disappearing through open doors, pulling things onto the floor and climbing everywhere while other patients tut-tutted and looked disapproving. It was no better in the doctor's consulting room – there was no sitting quietly on my lap. The consultation was conducted while pulling Gabriel out from under the furniture, making sure he didn't damage expensive instruments and trying to calm his screams.

No doubt the paediatrician had seen it all before and this behaviour only helped her come all the more quickly to a conclusion. At any rate she had no hesitation in giving her diagnosis: our son was 'severely mentally handicapped, probably autistic'. My heart sank. Faltering, I asked her what that implied and her reply caused my heart to plummet further. 'My dear,' she answered gently, 'you have a very difficult time ahead.'

We, or certainly I, left in a daze. Although half expecting to hear that he was mentally handicapped, we hadn't suspected autism. The truth had hit hard. Over and over in my head I repeated the words – mentally handicapped, severely mentally handicapped. Other words rushed through my mind, subnormal, brain damaged, retarded, idiot, cretin, all of them filling me with dreadful associations. I was ignorant about and had never had any contact with such people. One – or more precisely I – passed them sometimes in the street and barely gave them a second glance, lumping them all together and perhaps unconsciously not really considering them fellow human beings. Often misshapen and unattractive they shambled along, making funny noises or with their mouths open, even, oh horror, dribbling. Feeling vaguely ashamed, I'd looked away. Well, there could be no looking away any more.

Probably, I thought with a fragile optimism, mentally handicapped children were no different than other children – just a bit slower. Perhaps, as people said, they were very loving, very rewarding when you got to know them. (But Gabriel loving? rewarding? I couldn't imagine it.) Anyway, I told myself, it could happen to anyone. It was nothing to be ashamed of even if nothing to be proud of (I mean how could you be proud of a child like this?) And what about the future? What was his future? Or ours? No, it was better not to think that far, it was too daunting as one thing was for sure – mental handicap was for life.

As for the word 'autistic', although at the time, 1981, autism was a condition far fewer people had heard of, we had come across it. I had read an article about an autistic boy some years previously which had so horrified me I had never forgotten the chilling description of a passive and inert child locked into a silent and isolated world. By chance too we had read a book about autism: *The Empty Fortress* by Bruno Bettelheim (1967) in which he described children who were deeply unhappy, emotionally disturbed and alienated. However, the children he wrote about were not (permanently) mute, nor mentally handicapped and, according to Bettelheim, came from dysfunctional backgrounds. I couldn't match Gabriel up to these pictures of autistic children. Another reason I didn't recognise him in these descriptions was that he was much younger than the children I had read about and only just beginning to develop many of the salient features of autism. One must remember too that every child has his or her own definite character and that beneath the similarity of the autistic traits lie the differences of the individual.

Finally there was one overwhelming reason not to recognise Gabriel in Bettelheim's book, knowing he believed 'that the precipitating factor in infantile autism is the parent's wish that his child should not exist'. He blamed the condition of autism on cold unfeeling parents (mothers in particular, of course, who later became known as 'refrigerator' mothers) and we felt sure this couldn't possibly apply to us. Or could it? Had we gone wrong somewhere?

We were in fact confident we were not to blame for Gabriel's condition. Because of the epilepsy the cause appeared far more organic, yet the danger of this point of view was the seeds of self-doubt it sowed in the parents. One already felt guilty and inadequate however unjustifiably, and to be blamed for one's child's dysfunction was not helpful and only made a difficult situation worse.

The paediatrician's view was that the precise 'label' was not important and she urged us not to concern ourselves with it and to take up the offer we'd had of a place for Gabriel at a local school for the severely educationally subnormal. We were only too happy to agree that nothing more than 'mentally handicapped' was necessary. With hindsight I think perhaps we – and the doctor – were wrong as Gabriel might have had the benefit of specialist schooling sooner. But for the time being we dismissed the word 'autistic' from our minds and comforted ourselves with the prospect of some relief when he started school in the near future.

6

A cuckoo in the nest

We knew very little about autism or about people with learning difficulties then, but what we did know was that Gabriel was getting wilder. 'Wild' seemed the most appropriate word to describe so much of his behaviour, but in particular his complete imperviousness to all our attempts to relate to him – or maybe I should say to get him to relate to us – and to socialise him.

Sometimes when I talked about his ways to friends and acquaintances they would laugh and say 'Just like my dog.' 'But,' I would reply, 'you can teach a dog more than we have managed to teach Gabriel. You can toilet train a dog for a start. Teach it to come when you call, to sit when you want it to sit.' Sometimes it seemed a dog could understand much more than Gabriel could. At least it knew you.

Perhaps, we hoped, when he started school and had the benefit of trained teachers he might make some progress. At any rate, whatever happened at school I, for one, was extremely relieved that Gabriel would be 'off my hands' for a few hours a week. I was beginning to feel the strain.

He was three and a half and we were still very new to the tasks of looking after a child who by now was officially mentally handicapped. We were in receipt of Attendance Allowance, a benefit payable for looking after Gabriel. A doctor had been to the house to assess him. Without looking at me he had rattled through a questionnaire as if he'd been conducting market research for double-glazing – and with about the same amount of feeling. I gave the replies in a trance as he rubber-stamped the situation. 'Do you have to do this often?' I enquired timidly as I felt myself being labelled from now on 'mother of mentally handicapped child'. 'All the time,' he replied airily. 'There's an awful lot of them about.' And without a word of sympathy, commiseration or advice, he picked up his briefcase and breezed out of the front door leaving me to reflect on my new status.

Having just moved house to an area where we knew no one I felt even more isolated and Gabriel was getting more difficult. One of my chief memories of that period was that he began to scream as soon as he opened his eyes each morning and that one of us would have to leap out of bed instantly to try and pacify him and get him something to eat. 'What's the matter with him?' father-in-law asked in a perplexed voice when he was staying with us on one of these occasions. 'If only I knew!' I snapped, feeling desperate. For the problem was that we didn't know where to begin to console him; we had no idea what the matter was.

Shortly after we moved I joined the local contact group for families of mentally handicapped children and for the first time could compare Gabriel with other disabled children. I met several children with Down's syndrome and soon realised that, contrary to popular belief, they were not all the easy placid children I had thought them to be – if indeed I had ever thought about them – and that all of the children presented difficulties, more or less severe according to their conditions. Meeting these mothers and their children helped me to put my own problems into perspective, but I still felt that there was something about Gabriel that was more intractable and harder to reach. He seemed stranger and yes, wilder, than the others and however much the other mothers assured me that he would eventually become toilet trained and learn certain basic skills, and recounted incidences from their own lives to prove it, I was never convinced.

At this time too the situation was still so new to us that I had not fully accepted it. One day I was visiting an elderly neighbour whose son also happened to be there. I had Gabriel with me and as he crawled all over me and I tried to prevent him from creating the usual havoc I explained that he was handicapped. Suddenly, leaning forward confidentially, my neighbour's son asked, 'Tell me, is it true what they say, that having a child like Gabriel is a blessing? Do you feel that?'

I don't remember how I replied or even if I answered in words, but I'm sure the expression on my face was answer enough. A blessing!! This monster, this cuckoo in the nest who was taking over my life, a blessing? No, nothing could be further from the truth and nor could I seriously imagine that anyone could feel otherwise.

'But you love him,' an old friend insisted when I reported the incident to her. I hesitated. Did I love him? My feelings were far too ambivalent to be called love surely. Often bitter resentment filled me at the way my life had been ruined – as I saw it. Was that anything to do with love? Worse, if I were honest, I would have to admit I felt something closer to hate than love. How often I had wished this had never happened and I didn't have to endure such turmoil. Dreadful thoughts sometimes crept into my mind, like those of the mother of a Down's syndrome baby I knew who had written: 'There were times when I would return to his cot hoping that the breath of life had gone from him and we could resume our normal lives.'

I have always felt that this was one of the most difficult times with Gabriel and for any parent in a similar position – the period of coming to terms with it. Moving from being ashamed of it, resenting it, even wishing one's child had never been born, to accepting the situation takes time and distance. I was too busy feeling sorry for myself and railing against my fate (even if silently) to see it in perspective, and coming more and more into contact with Gabriel's world I still shrank from it. When he started school I had to wait for the school bus morning and afternoon with two other mothers. We often walked along together with our children and mentally I would pinch myself. No, this wasn't a dream; this was my child, I was here, now – undeniably and irrevocably part of this world.

A year or two later I was telling an acquaintance how I was faintly perplexed to find myself quite contented and happy with my life, despite the fact that Gabriel was not getting any easier. 'That's because you've accepted him,' she said wisely, and I realised she was right and what a difference that had made.

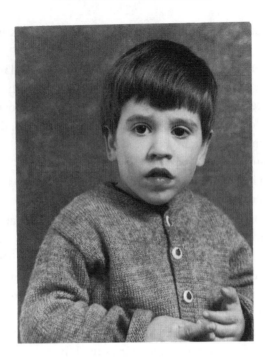

School photo; age 4. One eye looking through you and the other focused elsewhere

Gabriel has attended school since he was three and a half years old. Prior to that he had not been out of our sight for a single moment except when asleep and the attention he required was unremitting. When on very rare occasions people asked what they could do to help, I always replied without hesitation, 'Look after Gabriel for a couple of hours.' That was the best help of all – and now at school he was soon going to be looked after all day.

Since the early 1970s all children have had the right to be educated and even the most profoundly impaired children go to school. Before that time their daytime care came under the health service and little attempt was made to educate them.

'But what do they do at school?' people often ask – especially if they have been witnessing Gabriel charging around the garden mindlessly tearing up leaves, or trying to put both legs into the same trouser leg as he dresses himself. Well, learning to put one leg in each trouser leg is the sort of thing they learn at school. Children like

Gabriel have to be taught the simplest things – from learning to wash themselves to using a knife and fork (he still hasn't mastered either of these); from sorting blocks by colour to posting shapes. (These he can do but we haven't found any useful application for them.) All progress is unimaginably slow and many goals are frankly un- attainable. Yet this is not being pessimistic for the children do learn, some of them even succeeding beyond their parents' wildest imagin- ings, and who could wish for more than that? The teachers do a wonderful job.

Besides teaching new skills, school provides a structure and routine to the day – very important for all children but perhaps especially for those suffering from autism. Some order is established in their disordered lives. At school too Gabriel has to learn to be with other people. This is especially difficult for these children, one of whose principal problems is relating to others. Last but not least the children have a taste of many new experiences through school. The curriculum has always included trips and visits in the minibus and even getting on the bus and learning to tolerate a seat belt is part of their education. (Our boy utterly refused to be strapped in for many years, travelling in the boot or lying along the window ledge at the back of the taxi, to the consternation of whoever was driving.) Many of the trips may be apparently meaningless to Gabriel (a visit to an airport springs to mind), but many others provide useful social training as well as fun. These range from such simple outings as a meal in McDonald's (SIT at the table, no running around, that's enough ketchup THANK YOU), or shopping in a supermarket (NO grabbing), to visiting Father Christmas in Selfridges and holidays away from home. I take my hat off here to the staff for their efforts on all these occasions, none of which are simple at all with a group of children like Gabriel and his peers.

The school was for very slow learners and although we held out no great expectations we were determined to be open minded and optimistic. Surely they must be able to teach him something – if only to use the toilet or to sit at the table and use the cutlery instead of his fingers.

Art lesson – hand painting!

We were pleased to find that Gabriel settled in remarkably well. He seemed to like school. Certainly he never put up any resistance to going but always got on the school bus without a backward glance. This was a great relief as three and a half was very young (he was the youngest child there) and he might have hated it. It was also a relief as a few months after he started at the school I found I was pregnant again.

I was delighted to be having another baby if, understandably, a little apprehensive. Might I have another child like Gabriel? (Unlikely, but not impossible.) I was 42 so I had an amniocentesis and knew from that there was no possibility of a baby with Down's syndrome or spina bifida, but there is no screening for autism. The pregnancy and birth however were straightforward and troublefree and when Gabriel was nearly four and a half Jacob was born. Of course we scrutinised our new baby for signs of anything amiss and happily were able to detect none; in fact it was not long before we could see clearly how much Jacob differed from Gabriel. At only a few weeks old he looked at us, with intelligence and interest, and when we looked into his eyes he looked back. The difference was striking and we wondered how we had not noticed this sooner with Son Number Two for when you looked into Gabriel's eyes (which he resisted strenuously) he seemed either not to see you or to look straight through you.

The arrival of the new baby, strangely enough in spite of the extra work, made life with Gabriel easier – emotionally at least. It shifted the focus from him, lessened our constant preoccupation with him and rounded out the family. Christian too was very pleased to have what he referred to as a 'proper' brother. He was nearly nine and beginning to feel embarrassed about his other brother's funny ways.

We had wondered how Gabriel would take the arrival of the new member of the family but it hardly seemed to impinge upon him. We didn't notice any particular reaction and neither did the staff at school. There, like us, the teachers were optimistic and in a report written after he had attended for almost a year we read 'Gabriel is a happy little boy who soon became affectionate towards us.' According to his report, during the year his eye contact had improved; he had started to make progress in his toiletting; he 'now sits happily

Age 10 and playing fitting pen tops together – but attention caught by sunlight

throughout mealtimes'; he 'will obey a simple command' and 'initiate a game of peek-a-boo'. He also 'looked at a toy with interest', joined in playing the piano, and enjoyed finger painting, horse riding and sessions in the pool. Most amazing of all they reported: 'Much of his obsessional behaviour has disappeared and he is ready to co-operate in a structured setting.'

At home we tried to do our bit. We bought him a box of wooden bricks and tried to encourage him to build with them, but he never played with them imaginatively – all he did was arrange them either in a long line or balance them one on top of the other to form a tower. This last he could do quite skilfully, reaching a height of about three feet, but after a few months of lines and towers his interest in them was exhausted. I bought some large beads that could be threaded on a long lace and he showed great dexterity and quickly learned to thread them – but again he was not interested in making a necklace, say, or arranging the colours and soon tired of them too. He preferred to fiddle. The main problem seemed to be a total lack of motivation. He had none of the natural interest, curiosity or imagination of a normal child and neither could he be motivated by reward; he was equally indifferent to praise or sweets.

Soon his teachers were finding their initial optimism was not proving justified, or perhaps they had wished to see progress where there was none. Now they wrote: 'Gabriel still puzzles us considerably. We are looking for the key to get him to use his energy and skills in a positive manner.' Eventually after he had been at the school three years, according to his report he had made 'little or no progress' in his toiletting; at mealtimes he needed verbal reminders 'not to use his fingers' and also often spilled drinks deliberately to play with the liquid or 'lap with his tongue'. He still indulged in obsessive behaviours and although they endeavoured to 'take a firmly positive line with his obsessions' and distract him from these activities 'this increasingly leads to tantrums'. He had learned to dress himself but also to undress – and did so at the drop of a hat. Toys still held no interest for him and they observed that 'he rarely uses equipment in the way that it is intended'.

Most significantly there had been no development as far as language was concerned. Although his teachers had occasionally imagined his babbling included the odd word – we were told more than once he'd said 'hello' and one or two other words – this proved to be a false hope. Because of his lack of speech they were now attempting to introduce two or three basic signs to help him communicate but 'as yet he has not responded in any way to our efforts'. Finally a great problem, and one that was increasing year by year, was his 'taste for freedom and wide open spaces. He spends a great deal of time trying to climb over the fence and get out of the playground making close supervision essential at all times'; in consequence locks had been added to doors and fences raised.

On the plus side – well, what was there to put on the plus side apart from the fact that he had learned (or taught himself) to swim? According to the staff he was becoming more sociable, there was more eye and body contact, a greater willingness to join group activities (allegedly), and to sit at the table to work. But the fact was these improvements were not making him any easier to handle. He still escaped regularly and caused problems in the classroom and report after report referred to his stubbornness and disruptiveness.

Eventually an extra member of staff was engaged especially for Gabriel. (When the Head asked me what they should look for in applicants for the job I replied that besides patience and a good heart I thought stamina was the most necessary quality.) It was decided that his day should be spent in physical activity – swimming, trampolining, walks, etc., partly to keep him happy and wear him out and partly to remove him from the classroom and let the others work unhindered.

As far as we were concerned these new measures only emphasized how little progress our son was making. If they had to resort to this at age six and a half what would they do when he was a teenager? However, when I broached the subject with the Head she brushed my fears aside.

It was around this time we discovered by chance that there was a school in the county for autistic children. Ever since the time when the paediatrician had first suggested Gabriel might be autistic we had more or less forgotten about the label – as she had advised. It was true others had also suggested it from time to time and I had once tentatively asked about it at school, only to be told by the Head that Gabriel certainly wasn't autistic – whereas his class teacher had asserted 'we were all a bit autistic'!

Then one day I was in the supermarket at the checkout with Gabriel. Queues, like hospital waiting rooms, are usually a nightmare scenario as people with autism are notoriously impatient. My palms would begin to sweat if we had to wait more than about three minutes. This time Gabriel was causing a commotion, interfering in other people's trolleys and shouting, when suddenly a woman appeared at my side saying: 'Oh, I do sympathise, I know what it's like. I've got an autistic one too.' She told me about her daughter, some years older than Gabriel, who attended the school we had heard of.

So, we thought, perhaps we'd been wrong to forget about the label, perhaps it was important after all. If our son was autistic and there were special schools for such children, surely, we reasoned, he might make more progress there? We decided to investigate and made an appointment to visit the school.

The first thing we were pleased to note as we arrived was that the place was surrounded by a high fence and that all the doors had two handles – one at normal level and one at the top of the door out of reach of little hands. We were worried about Gabriel behaving badly, making it difficult for us to look round and talk to staff, but the Head assured us that all the children were, or had been, like him, flinging themselves about all over the place and never sitting down. She took his hand in an iron grip, marched him along firmly and took us on a tour of the school.

It didn't take us long to see the similarity between Gabriel and these children, many of whom were also mute and indulging in stereotypical behaviour. Observing this and talking to the staff we were soon convinced that this was where he should be and, after conferring with the Head, we decided to apply to the authorities for him to be transferred there.

7

New school

Gabriel was not yet 7 when we first visited the school for autistic children and decided to set about getting him transferred there. This, as many parents will probably not be surprised to hear, turned out to be no easy matter. Several reports had to be submitted to county and we had to be careful not to tread on anyone's toes if we wanted to get our way.

The first step was to establish the question of autism. Although the paediatrician we had seen four years previously had suggested autism, since then the word had hardly been mentioned – certainly not by all the professionals who had dealings with Gabriel – and now we needed confirmation. The school worked closely with a consultant in paediatric mental handicap and the Head wanted Gabriel to be seen by him before anything else.

Dr R was the most charming and sympathetic person we could have wished to deal with and could not have been more helpful. (The same could not be said for some of the other people involved in the negotiations.) I loved the way he referred to Gabriel as 'this interesting little boy' and 'this spectacular young man' in his reports and to us wrote how he 'had greatly enjoyed' seeing him. What a contrast this was to other professionals we had seen over the years who sometimes didn't even manage to spell his name correctly or in one case referred to him throughout as 'Gareth'. More than once we had been to consultations or received letters where Gabriel had been described as 'your daughter Gabrielle'. In these cases one can hardly value the opinion or advice of the professional concerned with respect to one's child and yet it is on these opinions that important decisions are made.

Dr R's opinion, which we did value, was that although Gabriel was 'more socially responsive, even provocative [tell us about it!] than would be expected in an autistic child', nevertheless he had 'rarely seen one with such unremitting and dedicated capacity to produce the whole repertoire of autistic skills and stereotyped behaviours to their full exasperating extent'. Why he was like this he hesitated to say, emphasising that as far as Gabriel's education was concerned it was not necessary to know whether he was 'a retarded epileptic child with autistic features or an autistic child with fits'. In his view the important point was that Gabriel needed the special education a school for children with autism would provide: a more structured day, smaller classes with a higher staff to pupil ratio and last but not least a secure environment.

Having confirmed that Gabriel did indeed suffer from autism or autistic features, it was now necessary to have reports from his present school, the school's medical officer and, most importantly, the educational psychologist. The appointments and reports took time and the process dragged on interminably until almost a year after setting the ball rolling we received a reply from county *refusing* to agree to a transfer. This refusal we felt was mainly due to the educational psychologist's report which had concluded by saying that she considered Gabriel to be correctly placed where he was. No mention was made of autism in her report, even though it transpired through the medical report that the audiologist who had tested his hearing three years previously had suggested autistic tendencies and that he should be referred to Dr R then – information which had never been divulged to us at the time. (Why not?)

We set about contesting the decision as by now we were determined that Gabriel should have the chance of specialist education. If we wished to help him as far as we were able we felt we had no choice but to persevere. One other consideration made us very keen to have him transferred and that was the fact that the new school had recently opened a residential unit and half the children spent from Monday to Friday there, only going home at weekends. Not that we wanted Gabriel to have a residential place yet, but we saw it as a sort of insurance should the need arise. More angry letters and cogent arguments were dispatched, with Dr R providing valuable assistance, and our correspondence file had almost reached bursting point when finally, to our great satisfaction and delight, we were informed that the decision had been reversed. Funding and a place for him at the school was confirmed and he could start the following term. He would be 8 years old.

So what was 'this interesting little boy' like in September 1986? In the educational psychologist's report written the previous year when he was 7 he was 'functioning between a 6 and 9 month level.' If that was the case (and we agreed it was) it was no wonder his teachers wrote he needed 'a great deal of help in all areas of the curriculum' as well as being 'solitary, withdrawn, extremely disruptive and obsessive'. Perhaps the area where least help was needed was the physical one. They reported that Gabriel was 'an attractive and agile little boy who walks, runs, jumps and skips with grace and skill. He vaults and climbs with ease.' (He had recently vaulted right over the side of a bouncy castle and made off with the speed of a greyhound, to give just one example of his prowess in this field.)

We agreed that, the physical side apart, Gabriel needed help with his most basic functions – eating, sleeping and toiletting – which impinged on family life to an almost intolerable extent.

His eating habits had always been unbearable, making mealtimes an endurance test rather than a pleasure. First, from the moment he was able to walk it was almost impossible to get him to sit at the table – he ate on the wing with one or other of us proffering a spoonful of food as he rushed past. He also wanted food when he wanted it – that was instantly – and not to provide it provoked screaming and tantrums. Perhaps we gave in too easily (with hindsight I'm sure we did) but as food seemed to calm him we were in no hurry to take a stand over it. Then there was the mess. He thought nothing of taking a handful of peanut butter – or chicken, or rice, whatever happened to be on the menu – and as he ran around he left a trail of food and sticky or greasy marks on walls and furniture. Drinks he sprinkled on the floor making nice little puddles to play in.

Even when as he got older he did sit at the table, Neil and I had to jump up and down so often to attend to him, wipe his hands, remove twirlers, mop up spills and admonish him for grabbing (not forgetting there was a baby too) that we couldn't relax or enjoy our own meal. To make matters worse Neil was suffering from a stomach ulcer.

Still we persevered in our attempts at a civilised evening meal, convinced it was an essential part of family life and that Gabriel should learn to participate. One day though when he was about 7, after a particularly chaotic dinner we decided we could not tolerate meals with an autistic boy any longer and that if we didn't do something we would all end up with ulcers. We resolved to feed him separately before we ate and then shut him in his room while the rest of the family had their meal.

This strategy worked surprisingly well. Gabriel could now have one-to-one attention at the table. I made an effort to prepare food he especially enjoyed so there was less likelihood of him messing about with it and there was no one else's to mess about with either. He also got to eat earlier so was not frustrated at having to wait and once his tummy was full he usually didn't mind being put upstairs in his room. It wasn't an ideal solution – we still couldn't linger, especially if there were sounds of protest penetrating the ceiling – but it was a vast improvement and the best we could come up with until he became sufficiently table trained to rejoin us. Perhaps the new school would bring this time nearer.

It was more difficult to find a solution to the problems which bedtime and sleeping presented, though at 8 years old he was usually asleep at a reasonable hour, by which I mean before midnight, and rarely up all night. He still slept in his bedroom then, which we had tried to make cosy and attractive for him, hoping for some subliminal effect – in vain I fear. He soon picked a huge area of plaster off the wall and pulled down the curtains so often that we left them down. The carpet he pulled up and unravelled. Eventually the room contained nothing but his bed and a tall cupboard. After he had pushed over the cupboard a few times Neil screwed it to the wall. He then took to climbing onto the cupboard and jumping off it, landing with a resounding thud. This he could keep up indefinitely. The plaster on the ceiling below began to crack. We removed the cupboard – and he began to jump off the window sill. To deaden the noise Neil bought enough thick foam to cover the floor and then covered that with carpet which he battened and screwed down at the edges. We removed the bed – he preferred to sleep on the floor anyway – and provided large floor cushions instead. The light switch was moved outside the room so he could not flick it on and off all night and the window was screwed shut except for a small gap for ventilation.

The long evenings took their toll. One has less energy and patience by that time of day and feels, resentfully, deserving of a little rest. One evening I snapped. Gabriel just would not settle. It was late. Thuds, knocks and shrieks were echoing through the house and the other two boys could not sleep. Thinking that I would make one last attempt at calming him I plodded up the stairs. I sat on the floor and started to sing softly but when he began to climb onto the window sill yet again, before I knew it I'd grabbed him and – forgive me Gabriel – I bit him. I didn't draw blood, but to my everlasting shame, I sank my teeth into his arm. There are no excuses for my reaction (which incidentally had no effect, calming or otherwise) as he couldn't help it of course. He was in the grip of his hyperactivity and simply unable to unwind. No, there was little we could do but grin and bear it and turn up the hi-fi to drown the noise. At least once asleep he never woke and we could count on peace and quiet till morning.

By contrast, although the fact that Gabriel was not toilet trained was a source of endless drudgery (even if lightened significantly by disposable pads and a washing machine), it was not so hard to put up with as the disturbed meals and the interminable evenings. Unpleasant yes, but not demanding physically or emotionally as, say, the sudden mood swings or desperate headbanging. I would rather change a dozen pairs of dirty pants than endure a Big Mood.

At 8 years old Gabriel was, as they described, a handsome boy – at least when he kept his mouth shut and one didn't see his exceptionally large gums and tiny teeth. This fact was very definitely to his advantage, his teachers assured me, for though beauty may be only skin deep it is difficult to appreciate that by the same token so is unattractiveness; most people react more favourably to those blessed with good looks. But handsome is as handsome does and though it might have helped when we were out and about and came into contact with other people, it did not make looking after him at home any easier. We had to fill in a questionnaire for the new school listing Gabriel's abilities and non-abilities, his likes and dislikes. They also asked us to list his most difficult features and his best ones. We had no hesitation in naming his hyperactivity and obsessiveness as the most trying characteristics and ones that precluded anything else. He wouldn't even learn to do up a button if he couldn't stop running and twirling for a few minutes.

Age 5 and the love affair with rubber gloves begins

This was the peak of Gabriel's Rubber Glove Period. We agreed with heartfelt sighs that if the new school achieved nothing more than weaning our son off rubber gloves it would have been well worth all the trouble of getting him there. It was exactly as one mother wrote: 'Just when you are relieved an obsession has passed another insidiously takes its place. Or an older one reappears with renewed vigour.' Some seem totally weird – such as a compulsion to put a foot on every ledge, wall or step of a particular height as we walked along – slowing our progress down the high street to a crawl. Many come and go and objects of desire have varied. Plugs and chains were a longtime favourite but blackened his hands and face. Dishcloths and tea towels were worse – there was never one to be found when wanted. Spitting on the windows and smearing the spittle enraged me and removing his brothers' shoelaces enraged them, but the rubber gloves got to all of us.

It was a fixation that lasted years and Gabriel would pass his whole day when not eating or sleeping, with rubber gloves. He flapped them and twirled them. He put them in his mouth – a complete pair – and pulled them out again wet and slobbery. He blew them up. He filled them with water until they burst, usually on the carpet, and tore them to pieces. He grabbed packets of them in supermarkets and snatched them off and out of anyone's hands, anywhere. Once as we were walking past a factory a white-coated laboratory worker emerged, casually holding a pair in his hands. A whirlwind in the shape of a small boy blew by, whisked them away and disappeared down the street leaving the astonished man empty handed and bewildered.

At home we were constantly seeking new hiding places so that we could have a pair intact. We barely managed to keep one jump ahead of Gabriel, who might be a slow learner in every other respect, but was a genius at finding gloves. Frequently we hid them so well we forgot where we'd put them. Yes, oh yes, we would be thankful to see an end to the rubber glove obsession – even knowing it would be replaced by some other fixation.

As for Gabriel's best feature, what could we put there? Racking our brains we finally decided his best feature was his 'mischievous charm' – for it's true that however exasperating he may be there remains something innately endearing about him. His provocativeness is allied with an innocence which, together with his contagious grin, charms despite oneself. We only hoped the staff at the new school would be equally beguiled by it.

Now Gabriel had a label. 'At least you know now what's wrong with him, that must be a relief,' people said, and they were right. There was a certain comfort in knowing, even if, when asked what 'autistic' meant, I was apt to reply 'it means *impossible*'. Now it remained to be seen how important the label was; how going to a school for children with autism would affect him and whether he would become more 'possible'.

One immediate improvement as far as I was concerned was not due to the skill of the teachers or the new environment but the fact that he would now be collected from home and transported to and from school by taxi. For the previous five years I had had to walk with Gabriel (and later Jacob) to the high street and wait for the school bus. It meant putting a harness and reins on Gabriel, which as he got older he vigorously resisted. In the end Jacob was at school himself. After being collected in the afternoon and brought home, twenty minutes later he had to return with me back to the bus stop to wait for Gabriel. How pleased I was to be relieved of all that hassle.

The improvement in my situation was unfortunately not matched by any improvement at school. Once again Gabriel was proving to be one of the most demanding and intransigent pupils and his first reports did not give grounds for encouragement. After references to his demands for attention, his stubbornness, his lack of effort and motivation, he was described by his teachers as 'a capable little boy who does not choose to involve himself' and by the Head as a 'non-conformist'. This last surprised me – I thought all people with autism were non-conformists by definition. How could it be otherwise and could words like 'choose' be applied to Gabriel?

On the other hand we were not surprised that their greatest problem with him was his obsession with rubber gloves. 'He ransacks classrooms in a frantic search for them,' they wrote and quickly made the rubber glove problem one of their priorities. After a few months they succeeded in curbing his addiction. Whether his ensuing passion for J-cloths – perfect for tearing and twirling – was an improvement was debatable.

The home/school book went back and forth with details of G's days, his progress and regressions. There were endless entries about toileting and mealtimes and his general behaviour. One Friday his teacher wrote how pleased she was with him, then finished: 'Only one bad incident this week – he ate the classroom goldfish. I went out of the room for a moment,' she continued 'and when I returned he had it in his mouth. I made him spit it out but it was already dead.' She wasn't amused, though his brothers thought it hilarious and another good story to tell their friends.

During the summer term a school trip to the coast was proposed and we were asked if we would like Gabriel to go. The offer of any sort of respite was music to our ears and at the thought of four whole days without the Wild Boy we jumped at it. This was a big mistake. In our haste to accept we had not thought to enquire about details and it turned out the children and staff were staying in caravans. For Gabriel to be cooped up in such a small space with a member of staff he didn't know must have been very alarming, even terrifying. One cannot know what goes on in such a seemingly confused mind but can only draw conclusions from his actions. He returned literally black and blue from having hurled himself about the caravan in an effort to avoid contact with his carers and had apparently spent most of the so-called holiday under the table refusing to budge. He had also developed a phobia of minibuses which persisted most incon-veniently for more than a year, perhaps imagining all minibuses everywhere were bound for a caravan site on the south coast.

The holiday resulted in Gabriel being 'totally unco-operative', according to school, and 'completely unmanageable, aggressive and withdrawn'. By the end of the summer term (also spent mainly under the classroom table) we were seriously worried they might refuse to keep him. We couldn't blame them and had to admit we ourselves were largely responsible for this unfortunate episode. I wryly remarked to Neil that so far our son's mischievous charm had failed to work its spell.

As a further result Gabriel was never to go on another school holiday – neither we nor the staff dared risk it (though he was able to join his peers for the odd day). In later years his name was not put forward for the school trip to Eurodisney, nor for tea at Number 10 with the Prime Minister's wife. However, more importantly, he was allowed to continue as a pupil and an impressive list of objectives was drawn up for the following year. Besides the usual toiletting and mealtime aims, the targets included learning to sign 'please, hello and goodbye' and understanding and acting on such simple instructions as 'sit down, stand up and come here'. They also hoped to teach him to keep his swimming trunks on in the pool and not to eat the materials – paint, clay, glue, plasticine – during the art lessons.

8

Growing up, or fitting a square peg into a round hole

So far the transfer to the new school had not resulted in any beneficial effects – in fact the reverse. After the ill-fated holiday Gabriel's behaviour had deteriorated noticeably. 'Are the other children as impossible?' I asked the staff desperately, but they wisely refused to be drawn into making comparisons – though I got the feeling they too sometimes felt pushed to the limits. Not surprisingly.

Visiting the school, which catered for about forty pupils, was like entering another world. The approach is down a leafy country road and one rounds a bend to see some low buildings surrounded by a seven-foot chain-link fence and a high secure gate. The children, if it is breaktime, are in the playground sitting on swings and slides, riding bikes or just running about – at first glance, like any other children. Then on closer observation one notices that they are nearly all boys; autism affects four times as many boys as girls. Looking again you realise that none of them are playing together. They aren't gathered in twos and threes but each seems to be moving in his or her own orbit, alone in his own world. The fact that about a third of them are mute adds to the air of isolation surrounding many of them. Looking more closely still you notice that several of the children are fiddling or flapping something – grass, a piece of clothing or their own fingers, while others are jumping up and down or rocking. One mother on her first visit, so she told me later, was shocked to see the bell around Gabriel's neck, put on to keep track of him. What sort of place was this that her son might be coming to? She, and we, were coming face to face with autism.

You park your car and perhaps one of the children approaches the fence. 'Hallo. You've got a red car, haven't you? That red car there is yours, isn't it? Your car's a Ford. It's red, isn't it?' Philip's favourite topic of conversation is cars and every time we see him in future he waylays us to talk about cars – but by then we have discovered that he is not the only child there fascinated by and only talking on one subject. Now that Gabriel was at the school we were beginning to find out more about this baffling phenomenon called autism.

We joined the National Autistic Society and started to read the society's magazine *Communication* and everything else we could lay our hands on. It seemed that autism and autistic tendencies could

Through a glass darkly…age 13. This picture appeared in The Independent 1.7.92

cover a mystifyingly wide range. There were those people with amazing talents, able to reproduce any piece of music after a single hearing, or to draw complicated and detailed buildings from memory. Others could calculate instantaneously what day of the week a particular date would fall on – but couldn't tie their shoelaces. This was the sensational side of autism.

'You're lucky then,' I was told once when I said my son was autistic, the speaker being under the impression all autistic people had some particular talent or mark of genius. In fact of course those are the exceptions rather than the rule and I didn't know then of a single child who fell into that category.

It appeared that there were others with autism who were of average or above average intelligence and even attended mainstream schools; yet the remaining three-quarters, like Gabriel, suffered from mild to severe learning disabilities and often also suffered other associated disabilities such as epilepsy, Down's syndrome or dyslexia. Most of these children had severe behavioural problems too.

'Is your son very difficult?' another mother asked me when I met her at some social event shortly after Gabriel had started at the school. The implication was they were all difficult, the only difference being in degree.

'Well,' I sighed 'his name may be Gabriel, but he's definitely no angel.' Quite the reverse in fact.

With Gabriel out of the house from 8 till 4 and Jacob now at school I was able to work part-time during the term. I got a job as a cook at a small residential school for girls with emotional and behavioural difficulties. It was hard work but was an outlet for my creativity (I loved cooking) and I valued my time outside the home as well as the ever necessary money. As far as I was concerned preparing a meal for 40 was infinitely less stressful than looking after Gabriel.

'I don't know how you manage – but I suppose you get used to it,' was a common remark made to us when people heard about life with Son Number Two and of course after nine or ten years we were used to it; we accepted the limitations on our lives and the enslavement to which we were bound. One got used to it like one might get used to having only one arm – learning to make do in all sorts of ways, even forgetting about it a great deal of the time, yet wistfully aware one was never going to become a concert pianist.

Yes, we'd got used to socialising separately; we'd got used to snatched pleasures during moments of respite; we'd got used to fighting laziness and exasperation; and we weren't expecting any miracles. We'd toughened up and were beginning to feel in control of our lives once more – and sometimes snatched pleasures were the best anyway. As for Christian and Jacob, although they felt they missed out sometimes because of their brother, having grown up with him and not knowing any different, they were used to it too.

At the same time our shared plight and the confines of our existence – we were always at home – made for a tight little family. Neil had in any case intended to participate in bringing up the children as far as possible, but Gabriel's autism made that even more of an imperative; he more or less needed one-to-one attention. So whenever possible, and especially during the holidays, Neil would work at home – sawing lengths of wood or making a piece of joinery while Gabriel enjoyed running in and out of the garden and workshop. Long curling shavings made good playthings, so did the fragrant sawdust that gathered in drifts under the bench (and found its way into the house). Neil could keep an eye on Gabriel if I needed to shop or go out. Meanwhile the other two boys were often around with friends and footballs or taking bicycles to pieces (Neil and Christian took up cycling seriously around this time). Neither activity was of any interest to Gabriel apart from occasionally spinning the wheels when the bikes were upside down for repairs, but he seemed happy just to weave in and out with his shavings or dishcloth, checking the visitors from time to time by feeling their clothes or smelling their hair and receiving a benevolent pat on the head or slightly embarrassed smile in return. Now and again he would remind us he was autistic by suddenly appearing naked or causing a disaster with the glue or, worse, by abruptly changing mood and howling and roaring with distress.

Daily existence had its surreal aspects and it sometimes felt as if we were living on the edge of a volcano – even if we were beginning to recognise when to expect an eruption. 'Children with autistic

Just can't stand still for a photo (Christian is also camera-shy)

Age 9 – Taking a break from wheel-spinning while Jacob helps Christian with his bike

conditions are totally egocentric,' writes Lorna Wing (a psychiatric consultant for the NAS and herself the parent of an autistic child) 'not because of deliberate selfishness, but because they have no concept that others have thoughts or feelings.' 'It is life as the only person in the world,' according to Donna Williams, 'or watching the world without a "you" in it.' Faced with this overwhelming egocentricity and inappropriate behaviour we, the parents, come up against our own limitations — our inability to control powerful feelings of frustration, anger or despair, yet having no choice but to carry on.

'I'm not a person, I'm just a hand,' I wailed one day as, without looking at me, Gabriel took me by the hand and pushed it towards the hi-fi — his usual way of indicating his wants. Yet I couldn't help laughing when he would sometimes take *my* hand to scratch *his* leg if he had an itch; when one wasn't exasperated by him one could appreciate the funny side.

And there often was a funny side. You couldn't help laughing as, refusing all help, he would battle to get into a pair of trousers *via the ankles*, or would appear with his Y-fronts back to front on top of his trousers, blissfully unaware that anything was amiss. One evening he seemed quite unconscious of the fact that he had his own shoe on one foot and an oversized brogue of Neil's on the other, even when he had to drag it along as he tried to run. For some inscrutable reason for several weeks he wandered about with a tea-strainer carefully balanced on the back of his neck. Walking along the street he casually picked leaves, shredded them and sprinkled them on his head and how I wish we'd had a video-camera the time he climbed onto the extension roof in his underpants to be found hanging by them from the gutter and forcing us to cut them off to free him.

Although I believe Gabriel had no idea why we found some of his antics and oddities so hilarious, he often seemed pleased that he'd been the cause of our laughter and the more we laughed the more he would smile delightedly at our reaction. As for us, laughter was the best antidote to feelings of negativity and stress.

I found it helpful to write about my feelings too. I started keeping diaries and wrote some short articles about Gabriel which were published in *Communication*. The first concerned his obsession for vegetation and I was surprised but comforted to find how many other families shared our problems. Several readers wrote that their child also had 'stripped every bud off the camellia bush this spring' or 'was into plants in a big way'. One or two had stories of children whose botanical interests had been channelled into drawing plants or gardening and made suggestions as to how we might do the same. Unfortunately Gabriel cannot be persuaded to scribble, never mind draw or garden, but the general opinion was that he would grow out of his obsession. Admittedly there were hopeful signs; he was getting better at leaving the flowers alone and sticking to grass and leaves.

Escaping was another subject I wrote about and here too we were assured by other parents this would probably change, even perhaps to its opposite — a passive slothfulness and unwillingness to go anywhere. If only, we thought.

Meanwhile Gabriel continued at the new school and his teachers and their assistants — each class had 3 adults to 6 or 7 children — and the care workers at the respite home all did their best to socialise him and teach him the basics.

It was a slow process demanding infinite patience, great change being beside the point for many of the children, and the teachers and carers too must feel frustration and despair as they struggle day in day out to help the children; to help them acquire a few useful skills, however limited; to overcome their irrational fears (fears we can't imagine — of buses, cats, pianos); and to help them make a little more sense of their incomprehensible worlds. At least if great change is rarely achieved small changes take on all the more significance. Teachers can feel justly proud when they have taught a child to use a knife and fork instead of hands, to put shoes on the right feet, or to sign 'drink' — it's simply a different scale.

When Gabriel started at the school the educational psychologist had written: 'It may be some years before he learns to come when his own name is called. At this stage he does not obey any verbal instructions, listen to any warnings nor comprehend if he is scolded.' Now, aged 9 he understood at last when his name was called that something was required of him, even if he didn't know what it was. Sometimes in a flash of inspiration he got it right and shut the door when asked. At other times he might respond to the same request by, say, bringing a spoon to us – and no doubt was baffled by our helpless laughter. One day he astonished me by finding and giving me the egg-whisk as I was separating yolks from whites preparing to make meringue – his fondness for meringue no doubt having imprinted the connection between whisk and whites.

Slowly, slowly progress inched along. After a couple of years of being banished to his bedroom he was considered table trained enough to join us again for the evening meal. Some accomplishments were a mixed blessing. At nine and a half he finally learned to turn a door handle, having only been able to operate a lever type hitherto. He had also cracked how to slide a bolt and at school they taught him to turn on the taps – though could not teach him to turn them off (like most autistic children Gabriel loved water). Nevertheless it was progress. We mustn't complain even it did mean we had to be more watchful at home and Neil had to add locks to doors where previously a bolt had sufficed.

Then best of all, definitely best of all, and the accumulation of years of effort on the part of the staff, they taught him to wee in the lavatory – and pull the chain! I'm sure they were as thrilled as we were. Prior to this Gabriel had often got through a dozen pairs of pants a day. Staff had insisted he would never be trained if he continued to wear pads and he'd set off for school each and every day with two or three complete changes of clothes plus a bagful of spare pants. He was 12 and at last reliably dry.

They plugged away at other areas of the curriculum. It appeared he had a natural interest in science according to his report at the same age, being 'very sensuous and enjoying water play and playing with soap. He explores most things on the Nature Table, though the tadpoles had to be removed.' (No doubt someone remembered the fate of the goldfish.) In Home Economics (National Curriculum Level Zero) the target was to spread a piece of bread and jam *without eating any jam from the jar*. In Maths at age 12 the aim was to teach him to build a six-piece tower with Duplo blocks. But as in so many things he was uninterested – except to examine or smell the blocks – and staff noted that 'his problem-solving skills come to the fore in real life; when he is motivated he is very talented and determined'. In other words he could work out how to reach a high shelf by finding a chair to place on a cupboard and stand on it to gain his objective. Or at home he'd sussed that if I was answering the phone or doorbell I wouldn't be watching him and it was the ideal time to get up to something. (Why did it take us so long to get a cordless phone? Such a simple solution.)

One constantly reiterated problem which the staff faced was that Gabriel hated adult interference or directions – something he shared with Donna who hated 'being told what to do'. 'He will not tolerate adult help,' wrote one teacher while another stated, 'He can do what he's asked – it's my directions he resists.' He wanted everything 'on his own terms' and was 'resistant to anything formally presented' as they put it – and found that only by approaching matters obliquely could they avoid confrontation. He was 'demanding'.

And so he undeniably was in the accepted use of the term, yet perhaps we have to put ourselves in his shoes. Looking at it from Gabriel's point of view he demands relatively little; it is all the surrounding adults – parents, teachers, carers – who are the demanding ones, who will not leave him alone but are always requiring responses which, to him, are mostly irrelevant. After all (he might think) what was the point of putting together a few Duplo blocks when all you needed to know was how to reach the biscuits or find a way over the fence. Why not eat the jam when you are spreading the bread? And why bother using a tissue to wipe your nose when a sleeve is so much more handy? Teacher can then wipe the sleeve, if she insists. Because of his autism he is incapable of seeing from our point of view and it is little wonder if he resists our demands.

But it was also little wonder that progress was slow. Sometimes sadly there was regression. After nearly ten years without suffering a seizure, unaccountably (though perhaps connected with puberty?) aged 12 Gabriel started to fit again. He also became more stubborn about further toilet training, refusing utterly all inducements to use the lavatory when he opened his bowels. On the other hand we were often told how good he'd been when taken out ('behaved impeccably at the supermarket today'), that socially he had made 'tremendous'

Actually smiling for the camera – though avoiding looking with one eye – and displaying his strange gums and tiny teeth

progress and again that 'eye-contact was much improved'. (True.) He'd made progress too in music, picking up tunes and humming them happily: Twinkle, Twinkle, Little Star and Oranges and Lemons. 'Odd,' Neil remarked, 'that he can imitate a melody yet never imitates words.' In his reports language was optimistically referred to as 'delayed'.

Then aged 13, in one Great Leap Forward Gabriel learned to sign 'please' by putting his fingers to his lips. This was a really useful skill – one that we used more often to signal 'yes' as in 'Do you want a cup of tea Gabriel? Say 'please' if you do,' and he would touch his mouth, or not. The teachers' next goal was to get him to indicate 'No' – but for some reason this proved to be far more difficult; nor could they teach him to point rather than grab. Whether these failures were due to his 'unwillingness to conform' as they put it, or to a lack of motivation, or to an autistic fear of relating is difficult to say.

Unfortunately as Gabriel started adolescence he became more assertive and disruptive not only at school but also at The Haven. There he was causing problems with his escaping, undressing, incontinence, bad behaviour at meals and an increasingly erratic sleep pattern which interfered with the other residents. At school everyone bent over backwards to accommodate him; he got more one-to-one attention, his timetable was adapted to his needs and he seemed to be getting everything on his own terms.

Yet in spite of all the trouble he put everyone to, by this time the staff had got to know and grow fond of him. He was even a favourite of some. He was 'a likeable boy with a will of iron and unflagging energy'; he was 'full of his usual mischief and bounce'; he had 'many endearing qualities' and 'keeps us on our toes and laughing'. Not forgetting too that like his peers he had no malice or falsity in him, did not lie or cheat or try to hurt others. In fact in those matters was truly angelic.

Gabriel was not only physically strong – he had no trouble moving the piano across the music room single-handed when he was a small 10-year-old and didn't like its new position – but his character was equally strong. Although this caused problems it also prompted admiration and liking. If he was anarchic, he was also canny, quickly checking if anyone was looking before skipping into the bathroom with a bottle of milk to add to his bathwater or taking a chance to squeeze out of the window. His liveliness might have been wearing but that same vitality was also attractive. Though he rarely initiated or accepted close physical contact, he would often come right up, his face only inches from yours with his huge infectious grin and, as one acquaintance put it on meeting him for the first time, 'A smile is still a smile'.

You just couldn't help responding with warm feelings for him.

9

'But the greatest of these is charity'

Yet I continued to be surprised that people should actually choose to work with our children. How could they choose work so full of frustration and drudgery and demanding so much patience; work with so little reward in the way of status, money or even hope; work that required a commitment to and involvement with not only the children but also their families?

Of course, as they would be the first to admit, it's different for the teachers, welfare assistants, care workers and others. They go home after work. They get paid for it. They are detached in a way parents can never be, but above all they are not having to get on with all the other tasks of everyday life – shopping, cooking, looking after their other children or pursuing their own interests – at the same time as attending to an obsessive, hyperactive, disruptive, devilishly mischievous and non-conformist IDIOT. (They would of course disagree vehemently with my use of that word.)

Nonetheless they show us a different perspective: 'He fascinates me,' one care worker told me. 'They interest me,' revealed another. 'I can't take it for granted any more what it means to be a human being.' 'I'm drawn by the children themselves,' Gabriel's teacher said. 'They have such difficult lives and I can't help admiring them and wanting to make their lives more bearable.' 'I don't see the disability but the character behind it – and their helplessness makes them all the more lovable,' replied another when I asked him how he could do it. 'There's no pretence about them. They are what they are.'

In other cultures and at other times those born different were considered to be specially close to God – like Russia's 'holy fools' –

and to be treated accordingly. Perhaps this idea still exists consciously or unconsciously and attracts others to them. Certainly many of the people I have met who work with these children, both paid and unpaid, find the work deeply satisfying and would not wish to do anything else – fortunately for us, for they are not only helping the children but they are sharing the burden of the families. The burden of our children is often too much for us on our own; we need help and they provide it and support us with unobtrusive compassion.

Saturday 5 March

We didn't take Gabriel down the town this Saturday as I had volunteered to rattle a box for Mencap's annual street collection today.

It would be quite possible to fill one's life with charitable coffee mornings, collecting bric-à-brac for endless bazaars, organising jumbles and barbecues, bungee jumps, barn dances and sponsored head shaves. I suppose there can never be too many fundraisers and it is a tempting way of doing something for one's child – as long as it doesn't take over one's life. A self-confessed cynic, sometimes too I have my doubts about the aims of the fundraising. Are trips to Disneyland anything more than sentimental conscience salvers? No doubt many of the children (and adults – both carers and cared for) enjoy them, but are they worth such vast amounts of money and effort? Do they know it's Disneyland (Gabriel wouldn't) and might the money be better spent otherwise than on 'the trip of a lifetime'? Maybe.

On the other hand, where would we be without the dedicated efforts of parents, and who know better what is needed and are prepared to fight for it? Gabriel's school would not exist without them for a start, nor The Haven. Every summer I thank heaven that the local Mencap society organises a playscheme in the town for three weeks when our children are looked after by (mostly) volunteers. We also occasionally receive benefits from local charities. Yes, we have reason to be extremely grateful to fundraisers, both past and present, and for this reason I am more than willing to help from time to time.

I arrive early (there are several of us collecting) and position myself in the prime spot – the doorway of the largest supermarket in our small town – and start rattling. People are mostly generous. Everyone agrees 'it's a good cause' and of course many have a relative, a neighbour or friend with a learning disability (as we are getting used to calling it) and are sympathetic.

I shake my tin a little harder and listen to whispered confidences: 'My sister's 60 and been in an institution for thirty years and now they're closing it down and she's being moved into the community. I'm worried to death'; or 'Mother looked after my brother at home until she was crippled with arthritis. It broke her heart to see him go into a home.' Some people recognise me and enquire after Gabriel.

A few yards down the street 15-year-old Alastair, whose brother has Down's syndrome, is also shaking a tin. He too stands in a shop doorway, artfully leaping to open the door for shoppers as they enter or emerge. 'They just have to give me something then,' he says, proud of this little ploy, and urges me to feel the weight of his tin. Definitely much heavier than mine – and I return to renewed efforts. Now, should I fix my eye like the Ancient Mariner on passing individuals willing them to give or should I gaze into the middle distance at nothing in particular so as not to pressurise them? As I ponder this, conscience pricked, a woman slips in a few coins saying, 'I've passed you twice now, I can't pass you a third time.'

After a couple of hours my tin is getting heavy and is nearly full; I even have a £10 note in it. ('There, but for fortune…' said the donor.) By now my arm aches, I'm feeling cold and it is time to give up my pitch to the next collector and return to my duties back home.

There things were brilliant. Gabriel very happy, smiling, laughing and singing. He was quiet in the morning but full of fun in the afternoon and had a grin on his face from ear to ear most of the time as he tried to get us to play with him. Oddly, although people with autism tend to shrink from close physical contact they often seem to enjoy it in the form of a game of 'rough and tumble' or 'chase and catch' and Gabriel is no exception here. He loves to be rolled about, bundled, tickled and sat upon, and doesn't mind how rough the treatment is. Squealing and laughing he will ask over and over for more, and though his brothers or his father are happy to oblige they usually tire before he does. A game of chase is even more fun. He rushes from room to room slamming doors to escape, or trying (ineffectually) to hide from the chaser, even racing to me for protection. He has no real idea of hiding and he is never the chaser but this is the nearest he ever comes to playing with us.

How different he seems on days like this, especially when, as recently, he has been so brooding and withdrawn. Today he was looking at us continually, smiling and laughing, relating in other words, and one can see all Gabriel's charm when he is in this mood. Ah! if only he were like this more often; for a brief moment he seemed just like any other boy. A good day.

Wednesday 9 March

Gabriel home after two nights' respite.

We always get a report from The Haven concerning his stay. This time they wrote he had been happy and lively, adding that 'unfortunately the liveliness continued all night'. They also reported that during the day he had been very 'co-operative' – a word I never ever imagined could be applied to our boy! So he is improving.

The staff always try to be optimistic and positive in their reports, even finishing each one with the words 'Looking forward to seeing Gabriel next time.' (Do they really mean it?) But however positive they are, knowing the difficulties he presents, we are nervous that one day they might tell us they can't take him any longer. Most of the carers are young and female and are not always confident about handling an assertive and physically strong teenager. Clients such as Gabriel make extra demands and require higher staffing levels.

Besides, one can never count on anything continuing. Social Services, Health and Education are constantly reassessing their ideas and methods, reorganising facilities and shuffling personnel, and everything depends on the all-important funding.

Only two or three years ago 'they' decided to cut back on respite in our area and families were devastated. It is bad enough when a facility doesn't exist, but when one you have is taken away it is almost worse. (We found that we had only been allocated five or six nights for the entire summer holiday.) Because this was something that touched all of us and because we all felt strongly enough about it to fight, parents were soon up in arms, calling meetings, protesting vigorously and supporting one another. The battle (yet another battle on our own and our children's behalf) was won on that occasion and all our respite reinstated. But we might not be so lucky next time, and then what? Don't they realise, that the better the respite the better we're able to manage and the longer we can keep our children at home?

This evening Neil thought of a new name for Son Number Two – the Badger, because he's always badgering us of course. He mostly badgers us for music as he likes to have some playing all the time. ('Does he like music?' is a common enquiry, followed by 'They usually do.') He doesn't show any preference for a particular type or piece of music (though one taxi driver swears he responds favourably to New Age). He just pushes someone's hand at the hi-fi and then wanders off, not even appearing to listen. However, as soon as one CD is finished he comes in from the garden or another room and tugs another hand back to the hi-fi to put on the next. If we refuse to play more he will ask again – and again, and again and again. Like a badger he refuses to let go; and usually we give in.

Monday 14 March

To school for an update about the new school, or college. The meeting attended by the usual half a dozen or so besides ourselves. Dates were arranged for the Badger to attend there, with a welfare assistant for half a day initially, then building up to a full day at the beginning of next term. Everyone is working hard to help but it seems there might be a problem with funding some extra support which may be needed for him. Oh no.

Thursday 17 March

Gabriel is starting on a new drug for his fits today. We have had to acknowledge that the various alternative treatments we have tried have not helped and it is time to accept the orthodox approach. We have been very fortunate to have such an understanding consultant over the past couple of years; it will be interesting to see what effect the new treatment has. Let's hope for the best.

Friday 18 March

A rare treat – Gabriel is at The Haven tonight, tomorrow and Sunday night and won't be home until after school on Monday, so we have a free long weekend. Wonderful! Of course we are glad for respite at any time but if it falls during the week on workdays and schooldays we can't make so much use of it, so this is a bonus. We decide to get right away and as soon as Jacob is back from school set off for Dorset.

Monday 21 March

Back last night feeling well and refreshed after a lovely weekend and ready for the Badger who returned this afternoon having caused no problems at school or The Haven and very quiet for once.

We had a reply today from the office which had cut G's allowance and to which we had protested. Capitulation and the full allowance to be reinstated and awarded indefinitely, though no explanation for events was offered. Another little battle won, but I wonder who decided it should be reduced in the first place and how many other families had accepted the reduction without query. Often those who need it most are those least able to fight for it – or sometimes just too weary to bother.

Friday 25 March

Came home from school like a hurricane this afternoon, rushed straight through the house, into the garden and climbed onto the fence ready to jump into next door's garden. Got delayed moment-arily by his (new) trousers catching on the fence, but broke free tearing them irreparably, landed directly on a beautiful clump of daffodils, and made for neighbours' aviary screaming with excitement at the chase – namely myself in hot pursuit, though not over the fence I hasten to add. Several birds must have suffered near heart attack before I got him away, chuckling delightedly at the consternation he had caused. The neighbours are very understanding and patient but this has been happening too often lately.

Saturday 26 March

Neil spent the morning raising the height of the fence by adding a trellis to the top. We now have trellises on all sides of the garden – including at the corner where he gets onto the single-storey extension at the back of the house. This is to keep Gabriel off our long-suffering neighbours' extension roof, which he can climb onto from ours.

An amusing incident took place when Neil put that one up last summer. He was just putting the finishing touches to it as Gabriel arrived home from school. The Lad took one look at it and realising instantly what his father was doing went indoors, selected the largest book he could find, returned and placed it on the back doorstep. Then, looking very meaningfully at Neil, he kicked it furiously out of the door. Neil is an avid reader and I'm sure Gabriel was showing his anger towards his father by taking it out on one of Dad's favourite objects. In the same way he often beheads a few flowers when he wants to get at me, and as a keen gardener I have to acknowledge he could find no more effective way to upset me. 'He's not stupid,' people say when they hear about these exploits, and I'm inclined to agree.

In the evening Jacob wanted to blow and paint an egg for Easter, which falls next weekend. This is just the sort of activity that is fraught with pitfalls when a certain person is about; the sort of person who is likely to pick up the egg and squeeze it or poke it to see what happens, or the sort of person who drinks the paint water then runs away with the brush. Usually these pursuits are best carried on behind locked doors. However tonight all was well, with just one heart-stopping moment when he picked up the finished egg to examine it – then very gently, and as if to say I don't know what you're worrying about, put it down intact.

Sunday 27 March

To Neil's mother for the day – one of the very few places we can visit with the Wild Boy.

I have explained elsewhere the difficulties of taking Gabriel anywhere – especially to other people's houses. Their homes, naturally, are not set up for a Gabriel, and for us it is such hard work making sure he doesn't interfere with their houseplants or tip out the aquarium or rummage through their fridge or drawers, not to mention the problems of changing his dirty pants in unfamiliar bathrooms, that it is simpler not to visit them. Gardens too are not generally Gabriel-proof nor doors kept locked, so that it's necessary to be even more alert than at home.

Family on the other hand are different. They know what precautions to take and are willing to put up with the inconvenience of our visits (such as removing the handles from the bedroom doors for the duration of our stay). Gabriel enjoys going to his grandmother's house. It gives him a change of impressions in his limited world, it is stimulating for him to have a day out and we often include a visit to the park, which he likes.

It is an hour and a half's drive which Gabriel also enjoys; he is very rarely any trouble in the car these days, happy to sit in the back with his seatbelt on now and no longer liable to land in your lap as you negotiate a tricky intersection. The days are past too when belongings were thrown out of the window as we sped down the motorway or he tried to open the doors. It is true he occasionally likes to fiddle with the gear lever, which can be alarming when you're doing 70 mph, but generally he is happy to sit and twirl. I guess the movement of the car is calming and removes his need to be constantly moving himself.

He enjoyed his day out – and especially the roast dinner.

Monday 28 March

A terrible evening. Had a major tantrum. His taxi driver said there had been a confrontation at school and that it took himself, escort and a male teacher to get G into the taxi. Escort shows me the backs of his hands and arms where G has dug in his nails and drawn blood in several places. Was still wild when he got home and roared around the garden until tea. Kept dragging the garden table up to the fence and making out he was about to climb over – standing on the table with one leg on the top of the fence and looking towards the house challengingly – just itching for a reaction from me. I ordered myself to keep calm, told him to get down and pulled the table away; two minutes later he was at it again.

He continued through tea in the same vein – eating abominably with his hands and literally stuffing as much food into his mouth at once as he possibly could, at the same time daring us with his eyes to remonstrate with him. (This reminds me that in his school report *ten years ago* one of the aims his teacher listed was: 'To sit at the table for the duration of the meal, to use a fork, and not to cram his mouth even when hungry.')

Some people who look after Gabriel (teachers especially) find these incidents extremely difficult to deal with, feeling he shouldn't be allowed to 'get away with' such behaviour and that one shouldn't 'give in' to him. They see doing that as a loss of face and tend to look at the situation in terms of winning and losing. Naturally, being the ones in charge they are very reluctant to ignore his conduct and, in their eyes, admit defeat.

I sympathise as I share the same feelings; it is easy to get locked in a power struggle and difficult to be forced to relinquish one's authority or, more precisely, to realise how little one actually has. In our experience though, a confrontation is rarely productive. We are not dealing with a reasonable human being or one who makes connections between cause and effect. He has little control over himself at any time, even less when in the grip of one of these moods, and a head-on collision can make a potentially violent situation worse. We decided to ignore his behaviour.

Neil had planned to go out this evening and was in two minds about going by 7 o'clock but I assured him (and inwardly myself) that I could cope.

I tried playing some gentle music in an effort to calm him, but to no avail. Suddenly he jumped up and began to rush through the house from the back door to the front door, backwards and forwards, backwards and forwards. He threw himself against the back door and kicked it in fury. He screamed as loudly as he could – so loudly that he must have been heard at the other end of the street and Jacob had to put his hands over his ears. He banged his head against the wall and hit it with his fist and slapped his thighs as hard as he could. But nothing made him feel any better.

He tried to go out in the garden but it was dark and wet out there and I had locked the back door. He wrestled with all sorts of implements including the potato masher in an effort to open it but without success. By now he was ready to explode with rage and started to tear up Neil's cycling magazine. When Jacob took it away he got madder and went into the kitchen, picked up a tray and swung it round, knocking everything off the counters. I had just made myself a sustaining pot of tea which he picked up and hurled on the floor, then stood in all the tea leaves and boiling tea (a lot went over his feet and it must have hurt a bit) and howled. There were tea leaves everywhere, all over the floor, me, Gabriel, the walls and even the ceiling – and *still* he felt mad, until with a final flourish he tore up Jacob's maths homework. After that he felt a little better, although he sat crying and growling for another half an hour.

By the time Neil came home he had exhausted himself and his father gave him a nice hot soapy bath and wrapped him up in a warm towel while I cleared up and made him a big dish of his favourite cereal with lots of sugar to replace his lost energy. After that he was only too happy to get under his duvet get his head down and go to sleep.

Life is very hard when you're autistic.

Tuesday 29 March

Had a fit in the night – as we were not surprised to discover this morning, so of course he couldn't help it yesterday, poor chap, it must have been pre-epileptic tension.

(We have long recognised that Gabriel is frequently very tense and 'hyped up' prior to a fit. The seizure seems to release the tension and when he eventually comes round – always after a prolonged and deep sleep – he is invariably much calmer and happier. For this reason one doctor who used to treat him took the view the fits were cathartic.)

Had to stay at home to recover, which was just as well as we heard later that another child in his class had pushed in a large double-glazed window which had fallen on the teacher, knocking her unconscious and necessitating a visit to hospital. I didn't feel quite so bad about Gabriel's behaviour at school after that. Life can also be quite hard when you're a teacher in a school for autistic children.

Wednesday 30 March

End of term. Gabriel came home with an Easter card for us, supposedly made by himself, and some rather battered chocolate eggs in a by now very bedraggled nest. I don't know how the staff find their patience, I really don't. There was also an egg for him from school and another from the taxi crew – and he probably won't eat either of them (Jacob will though!). They are all very good hearted and kind to think of him and seem to be genuinely fond of him, however irritating he may be and however little return they get.

Was in a very giggly mood all evening which made a nice change and several times sat himself on Christian's lap. Later he insisted on sitting next to his brother (who is back home from university for a few days) and kept looking up at him laughing – obviously he's not entirely indifferent to us and Christian is definitely one of his favourites. Hope the good mood lasts – he has almost three weeks holiday from today and as usual I am feeling apprehensive at the prospect, even though I know from past experience that we'll probably manage without too much difficulty – and with a little help from our friends at The Haven. Gabriel will have a couple of short periods of respite there (two nights each time) but will be home for Easter weekend, which means we will too, and since we'll be at home we've invited two of the boys' cousins to join us. Gabriel seems to enjoy it when we have visitors and I suppose it's a change for him too.

Easter Sunday

One of the cousins organised an Easter egg hunt for the younger children. There are eggs for Gabriel but he is totally oblivious to the entire proceedings. Hasn't a shred of interest but just sits in a corner twiddling with his back to the others as they rush in and out searching for clues. In the afternoon we took a walk to the local monument, the remains of a castle, and Gabriel suddenly waded across the moat although there was a bridge only feet away. Typical. He was soaked up to the waist and although the sun was shining it was none too warm, but he seemed as oblivious to the wet and cold as he was to the egg hunt. What a strange boy he is.

A few days later we had a visit from some of my cousins, one of them exclaiming several times 'how sweet' he was and 'how communicative' he'd become since they'd last seen him some years previously. He had a good smell of all of them when they arrived and gave them a few of his funny little furtive looks. I have to admit that he behaved remarkably well throughout – hardly snatched anything at the table. It is good to be reminded how he appears through others' eyes sometimes – my cousins were quite taken with him.

I wasn't taken with him the next day however, when he managed to overcome the trellises and climbed onto the roof and – worse – the neighbours' roof. It is not a very strong affair, being made of corrugated plastic and not intended to support the weight of a jumping teenage boy and certainly not that of another person trying to reach him. Defiantly he took himself to the furthest corner and flatly refused to come down. Pleading, coaxing, bribing (packet of chocolate buttons), demanding, threatening (big stick) – all attempts to get him down were like water off a duck's back. It was much more

Family group. G as usual being restrained for the camera. Myself centre. In front of workshop with trellis to stop G getting onto the roof

fun to stay up there and see us all, though especially me I suspect, helplessly wringing our hands.

If only Neil had been at home. Gabriel usually obeys him. His father has a presence that he respects to some degree and Neil is the only person who has any real control over him. At last after half an hour or so he decided he'd had enough and came down and to my great relief no damage had been done – apart from to my nerves, which after two weeks of holiday were getting a little frayed. Tomorrow Neil has arranged to work at home. Hooray!

Thursday 14 April

Neil looks after Gabriel in his own way. First he locked the back door so that Mr Messy couldn't charge in and out of the house treading mud and sawdust everywhere and scattering torn leaves and shavings in his wake – fraying his Mum's nerves even further. He then tried to get him to work, that is to help his Dad to unload his van which is at the front of the house and carry wood and tools round to the workshop at the back. He hopes Gabriel might one day find a niche for himself somewhere putting things away or sweeping up, or who knows what. (One teacher suggested 'office shredder' as a career.) But Gabriel, like most teenage boys, is lazy. Carrying a saw from the van to the workshop he sits down halfway, distracted by a shaving he has found. He doesn't seem to understand what is required of him either and after carrying a length of wood to the shed as instructed, he then carries it back to the van. All at once his attention is caught by a clump of dandelions in a neighbouring garden and he drops the wood and shoots off up the street to grab a handful of leaves. Neil hauls him back and hands him another length of wood. He has to pass down a narrow alley to reach the garden but instead of turning the wood lengthways to get it through he walks bang into the alley with the wood across it. The effort of figuring out the next move is too much and he runs off again. Finally, with the van unloaded, Neil locks the garden gate and sets to work while Gabriel makes mincemeat of the lawn.

It was freezing cold with hailstorms and showers but they stayed out there all day (Dad believes in bringing them up tough). By 5 o'clock it looked as if 25 rugby scrums had taken place on the grass and as if Gabriel had been in the thick of all of them. He was plastered in mud from head to toe, but he'd enjoyed it. He was very happy all evening and, healthily tired from rushing about in the cold air, was asleep by 11 o'clock.

Only two more days now of the holiday and as usual it hasn't been too bad. He's been a good chap really, apart from the odd incident – and that's not his fault. As Neil remarked, 'You've got to admire the way he himself copes with his far from easy life.'

10

Many happy returns of the day

Monday 25 April

Gabriel's birthday, 16 today.

'Does he know it's his birthday?' people ask.

'Not as far as we can tell,' I reply. He shows no interest in his cards – sent faithfully by one or two aunts and his grandmothers (cheques enclosed), plus one from The Haven. By now everyone has given up sending presents. It's quite apparent that his desires are as limited as his intelligence – he wants nothing more than a full tummy, a warm duvet, music on the hi-fi and something to fiddle with.

Still, we have bought a new CD – one the taxi driver recommended though I don't know if it will register. I could buy him something to twirl (I have done in the past), but he seems to prefer to find his own twirlers and would probably reject mine. It wouldn't smell right. So the best I can do is to prepare one of his favourite meals even if he doesn't know it's a birthday treat. I'll cook lamb chops in a tomato sauce with plenty of rice, roast potatoes and salad with home-made raspberry ice-cream for dessert (we feed him well.) And I'll try not to let him wind me up today.

But that's easier said than done. As soon as he got home from school he rushed up to his room. I had persuaded Neil to put a chain on his window yesterday so that it could be opened a little more but not too far. It took Gabriel about two minutes to wrench off the chain and get out and onto the neighbour's roof – again. Could feel my blood pressure rising instantly as I struggled to hold my tongue. Yes, it's been a long 16 years.

'Does life with Gabriel get any easier as he gets older?' they ask.

'Well, yes,' I reply hesitantly, 'yes.' Our Wild Boy has become tamer with time and more stable. Life is not lived quite so much on the edge of sudden mood swings as it used to be and we have become more inured to them when they do occur. Also, imperceptibly but undeniably, he has s-l-o-w-e-d d-o-w-n, and that's a tremendous improvement. When a friend said years ago that no one could keep up his level of activity indefinitely I didn't believe her – but she was right. (Parents of young hyperactive children take heart.) Last but not least he understands more, and that is something which is increasing all the time and can only make life easier both for him and us.

I hesitated because with age new problems have arisen. Gabriel is bigger and stronger now and I, for one, can no longer control him physically; not only I, but also many of his carers. New behaviours have developed with age too and have to be tackled. Masturbation is one; he has to learn he cannot indulge in it wherever he pleases. Then there are things which haven't changed but have become more onerous over the years: it is one thing changing a dirty nappy on a 3-year-old but quite another attending to a 16-year-old. And some things have got worse: the late nights have got later. The fact remains though that we do experience our life with Gabriel differently from say ten years ago and it has become easier mainly because we understand each other a little better.

But to return to the birthday boy. I'm sure he enjoyed being the centre of attention all day. He had a birthday treat with his classmates of sausage and chips in the park (It's not a bad life sometimes, is it Gabriel?) and later there was a cake and candles and the whole school sang 'Happy Birthday' at assembly. Then back home there was a lovely dinner followed by balloons, unlimited chocolate buttons and lots of chasing and rough and tumble, new music and all rounded off with an extra dose of bubbles in the bath and no complaints about all the water on the floor.

Perhaps he did know it was a special day after all.

Wednesday 27 April

Came back from school with – oh no – a book of raffle tickets for me to sell. It seems I have only just finished selling the last lot. It's endless. Escort said he'd 'had a wobbly' in school.

Friday 29 April

Still wobbly. Went to new college (of further education!) for his first trial morning, accompanied by a member of staff from school. When he came home he was dressed in different clothes – obviously from the school supply of spares. The escort raised his eyes as he handed me a plastic sack of his own sodden clothes and his home/school book – from which I quote: 'The visit went well – he only pinched a few students, scratched members of staff and jumped in the lake.' (They had visited a park as part of the exercise.) 'Otherwise he was fine.' Oh dear, will they be able – or willing – to cope with him even though they said challenging behaviour was not a problem?

Bank holiday weekend

Quite a pleasant weekend. Weather wonderful and Gabriel happy to spend time in the house and garden; this is another way in which life with him has changed for the better. For many years we felt compelled to take him out for a long walk every day and often twice a day during weekends and holidays. (However much we like walking, we're not so keen on a cold winter's evening.) It was one of the best ways of calming him; the steady rhythm of walking seemed to have a settling effect on him and also gave him a change of impressions. As he has slowed down however the need has faded and he no longer drags us to the door or hurries to find his coat at the mention of a walk, although he still likes one when he is in the mood.

Was in Escape Mode through most of Saturday, once getting into the street and from there into another house, where he helped himself to some chips the man of the house happened to be eating and then as he ran off he spotted a sausage in their dog's dish and ate that too – to the mixed consternation and amusement of the neighbours. Naturally he was well pleased with that little escapade, smiling to himself and letting out exuberant whoops through the afternoon – no doubt at the memory of the sausage. This is the sort of thing he does to amuse himself – and the sausage was an unexpected bonus.

On the Monday afternoon in Rummage Mode again. Opening cupboards, peering under chairs and lifting up cushions, all very purposefully, looking for – looking for *what?* We have no idea, and maybe neither has he. It's another mystery concerning Gabriel we'll probably never know the answer to.

Tuesday 3 May

Now that Gabriel has turned 16 – and a moustache is appearing on his top lip to prove it – the state benefits system changes. He must now claim benefits in his own right – though of course we have to do it all for him. I spent all day making phone calls and struggling with the Department of Social Security – and now know why some call it the Department of Total Obscurity. There are forms to be filled in (one has 40 pages) and I must arrange to get a letter from our GP confirming Gabriel cannot read or write which is why he needs an appointee (myself) to deal with his affairs. (Would have thought it was obvious by now.) Fortunately because of my contact with the local support group and with people who have been over these hurdles already I am more conversant with the rules than some of the people I speak to on the phone. It's all very time consuming.

Thursday 5 May

Dropping him off after school the escort reports 'Has been as good as gold'. Two days running. In fact he has been generally quieter the last few weeks – quite sleepy at times. Could it be the drug he is taking now for his epilepsy? We know that drowsiness is one of the main side effects.

Monday 9 May

Should never have written the above. Have had three late nights in a row – one when he was up all night and we haven't slept in our own bed since Thursday. Bastard!

Thursday 12 May

'Very sleepy' when he came home from school according to the escort, and indeed he was for an hour or so. Then he disappeared upstairs and shortly after a rhythmic thumping could be heard coming from his room. At last I think he's getting the idea that his bedroom is the place to masturbate. Fortunately so far Gabriel's sexuality has not presented any problems. The masturbation is fairly intermittent. He seems mildly curious if he sees me naked and once or twice has reached out a hand to prod a breast, but in much the same way as he might, say, touch an animal's tail – to see what it feels like, and his curiosity has gone no further.

His urges satisfied or more likely evaporated he then spent a long time in the garden. My bike was out there which he sort of sat on and sort of walked round on very ineptly. He has no idea of balancing on a bicycle. There was also a trike in the garden (home from his school for Neil to repair) and he sat on that too – but he barely seems to make the connection between turning the pedals and moving forward. It's too much effort and he's completely unmotivated. But probably because both Christian and Neil are keen cyclists and he sees them cycling from time to time he likes to sit on one of the bikes. Riding a circuit of the school playground is one of the objectives his teacher is aiming for. Lorraine says he can almost do it, but adds she wishes 'he would open his eyes to steer'.

He is very clumsy in his handling of the bike too and spent about twenty minutes trying to prop it up against a wall, having made it very difficult for himself by trying to balance the basket on the saddle at the same time. When Neil came home, after asking 'How's my favourite?' he gave his favourite a push round the garden on the bike, but passing the apple tree some interesting leaves caught his eye and he took both hands off the handlebars to pick them and fell off.

Saturday 14 May

Had a fit last night and was tired all day. So far the new medication has not made any difference to the seizures. The dosage has been increased since he started on it but that hasn't had any effect either. We'll just have to be patient.

We went shopping with him anyway – and had a little altercation with someone. Gabriel had made some marks with his dirty hands on madam's front door as we passed her house. Criticising us for lack of discipline she launched into an attack.

Most people are very understanding when, after some inappropriate behaviour, we explain Gabriel has learning difficulties, he's handicapped, autistic, two cans short of a six pack – or whatever expression is the most appropriate at the time. But on rare occasions someone is unpleasant or unkind. 'Pick those up, slob,' a man told Gabriel once as he dropped some leaves in front of his gate when the two of us were out for a walk. Deaf to my words he continued to abuse us as I tried to tell him about my son. (All of this was lost on *him*, of course.) Torn between bursting into tears at his hurtful words and punching him, I did neither – but that was one day my skin grew a little thicker. This morning there was luckily no need for that, madam hastily apologising after Neil's exquisitely polite and cringe-making explanation.

To help at a jumble sale in aid of autism in the afternoon. Several people with autism there – sons and daughters of the organisers and supporters – all jumping, flapping, shouting, lungeing (at the refreshments mainly) or like one, quietly rocking and 'purring'. The money was to be used towards a Snoezelen room at a local day centre for young autistic adults. This is a room equipped with devices to 'provide a pleasant and relaxing sensory experience'. The room is dark while soft coloured lights play to form patterns and shapes which constantly change to soft music or, for example, to sounds of running water. The clients lie or sit on large floor cushions as they enjoy the stimulating or soothing effects. Needless to say a Snoezelen room costs loads of dosh.

Sunday 15 May

Tired all day. Awake all night.

Monday 16 May

Full of energy this morning even though had been running around all night. Just as 'high' (as teacher puts it) after school. Couldn't bear eating with him this evening with his hyped-up vibrations so we shut him in the garden with his dinner while we ate ours and watched him through the window. He didn't mind, just charged up and down and ate on the wing. Still running at midnight after *more than 40 hours awake* and we fell asleep before he did.

We have had many attempts to regulate Gabriel's sleep pattern over the years but have (obviously) had little success. In despair Neil once tried waking him at 6 o'clock every morning and taking him out for a walk to keep him on his feet before school but the interference of the fits meant it was impossible to do this for more than a few days at a time and anyway he was still full of life at night while we were tireder than ever. Like many autistic children it seems, he is always much calmer (and difficult to wake) in the mornings and gets more and more lively as the day progresses, ending up unable to switch off or unwind.

Tuesday 17 May

Still high after school, flopping about and laughing hysterically. Laughed so much while he was eating a dish of puffed wheat he blew them all over the room. Five minutes later was screaming and headbanging. Early night.

Wednesday 18 May

Comatose.

Thursday 19 May

Two members of staff from new college to school to observe Gabriel. Lorraine reported he had been 'super' and that they had been 'most impressed by the skills he has'. Really? She didn't specify which skills

– must ask her at the school Quiz Nite on Saturday. 'However,' she continued, 'they have concerns about him joining their unit as he is so mobile', though she reassured us that there were no problems about a place for him. Didn't feel very reassured.

Friday 20 May

Christian home for the weekend.

When we knew some months ago Jacob would be going on a school holiday next week we put in a request for respite for Gabriel at the same time and he was allocated five nights at The Haven. Christian is going to take over for one other night so Neil and I have almost a week's holiday together. We have booked a cottage in the Dales.

As well as making sure one does not neglect the other children in a family like ours, it is equally important for a couple to find time for each other. It is all too easy in any family for parents to be swallowed up in the endless cares and responsibilities of looking after young children and running a house and home. This is even more true when one of the children has special needs and over the years we have made the effort to get away on our own – sometimes just for the day, but a few times we have been able to go off for several days.

The longer breaks have mostly been thanks to my sisters and sister-in-law who have come and taken over house and boys – including Gabriel – once a year for the past three years, an edifying and memorable experience for all of them. I don't think they'll forget the time he ate the bar of soap they were bathing him with, or when he escaped naked in the rain and got onto the garage roof, and certainly not the time he made them run for several hundred yards over the common before he allowed himself to be caught and panting they all realised that they hadn't actually *run* anywhere in years. Of course he took the opportunity to be his most 'obstrop-olous' self.

Christian at least knew the ropes and we set off on Sunday morning leaving him in charge until Gabriel left for school and The Haven the following morning.

We rang our eldest when we arrived in the evening – he'd changed Gabriel four times, otherwise all was well; we could put our minds at rest and enjoy ourselves. The cottage was cosy, the position perfect and the weather wonderful. We fell in love with the Dales – and again with each other.

Am I my brother's keeper?

'When I grow up,' Jacob said to me one day, aged about eight and four years Gabriel's junior, 'I want a family just like ours: three kids, one of them handicapped.'

'A handicapped one!' I exclaimed laughing. 'Why?'

'Because,' he replied, as if it were obvious, 'I like Gabriel.'

People often ask how Christian and Jacob feel about their brother – frequently adding 'what a shame' it is and how difficult it must be for them; on those occasions I like to recount this conversation. Sometimes I might also tell them that a few days after our little exchange Gabriel was having a screaming session and I asked Jacob if he would still like to have a handicapped child. This time the reply was a thoughtful: 'I think I'd rather have a dog.'

It is inevitable that parents worry about the effects a child with a severe impairment has on the rest of the family. Such a child makes enormous demands on their time and energy and they wonder if there will be enough left for the others. Might their other children feel left out or suffer? I have to answer that almost certainly they will – but with the proviso that this is not necessarily cause for alarm.

In some cases where, for example, the autistic or handicapped child is one of twins or very close in age to a sibling, the brother or sister may manifest quite disturbed behaviour and obvious negative effects – and then parents have a double burden on their hands. But extreme adverse reactions are not the case in the majority of families and according to an article in *Communication*: 'Generally, brothers and sisters of children with handicaps show little resentment or hostility, they do not exhibit more behavioural or emotional problems, and indeed may grow up to be more altruistic, supportive and sensitive than their peers.'

Walking the towpath with Jacob and Christian. Eye down as ever and a handful of grass

Refusing to co-operate for a photo with his brothers

How the disabled child affects any siblings depends on many variables including the age and number of children in the family and their level of understanding as well as the extent of the impairment. Perhaps the over-riding factors are the attitudes of the parents and the individual characters of the children.

Taking my own family as an example of the last point, behaviour that made one brother cringe with embarrassment provided the other with a source of funny stories, and what would frustrate or anger one might leave the other indifferent.

A lot of Gabriel's behaviour was embarrassing – for a start he was liable to undress himself at any time and anywhere. If you had friends round he was likely to sniff at them or whisk someone's chocolate bar out of their hands and eat it. As he ran back and forth with his bits of string and rubber gloves making incomprehensible noises, what did you tell your friends?

Understandably, for a child who does not like to draw attention to himself to have a brother like Gabriel can be agonisingly embarrassing – especially if you are at that awkward age when everything from what car your parents drive to how they dress is a potential source of discomfort. However, with growing confidence and maturity these are not usually problems that endure. It turns out that, after their initial surprise or curiosity, your friends accept Gabriel's (and your parents') funny ways quite naturally and do not think any the less of you for them.

There is no denying though that whatever one's character or attitude, life can be painful when Gabriel is around. We all get upset by his big moods, especially when he is very distressed or shedding tears. Self-injurious acts are painful to witness and screaming and shouting are difficult to ignore. Seeing someone in the throes of an epileptic seizure can also be profoundly disturbing, above all for a child. Add to this the fact that he cannot tell us what the matter is or how he feels and our feelings of pain and helplessness are increased.

We are seeing suffering, or so it appears, and can't help suffering ourselves. However, I feel compelled to say here that in my view this is not necessarily a bad thing. Suffering is an intrinsic part of life which cannot be avoided and while no one would wish on another the kind of pain that leaves a person indelibly scarred, there is also suffering which leads to greater maturity and understanding.

Over the years since Gabriel was born I have met numerous families with a handicapped child, autistic or otherwise, and have been impressed many times by the mature and loving attitudes of brothers and sisters – a fact we parents often comment on to each other. There are always a few of them helping out on playschemes, outings, school events, fundraising and so on. They don't have to do these things, they choose to.

Many take on some of the responsibilities of carers – help to dress the disabled one, teach them simple skills or look after them when parents are out. Although most parents agree it is not 'fair' to expect their other children to help, probably in the majority of families siblings are encouraged and do help in much the same way they would with normal brothers and sisters. Some are very protective towards their less able sibling while others go on to train as professionals and work with the disabled or disadvantaged.

More than once I have been told by siblings, my own children included, how they get irritated by people who appear to patronise them by being 'too sympathetic' or 'pitying', when the brothers and sisters themselves see the situation as no big deal – the disabled child, though admittedly a bit of a nuisance at times, is simply another member of the family. There are some children too who even enjoy the notoriety of their disabled siblings. I am reminded of one who hadn't accompanied his mother and autistic sister the day she set off the fire alarm in a major DIY store. Hearing later about the ensuing chaos he sighed ruefully, 'Oh, if only I'd been there.'

Of course there were certain activities the other two couldn't enjoy, but then equally there were activities we couldn't enjoy for reasons such as lack of money or time. At the same time we did make an effort to compensate, to arrange treats and outings when Gabriel was away; we did our best to give them as much time and attention as possible because of him.

It is true that in their everyday lives they have always to remember their brother. To remember not to leave schoolbooks around in case pages are torn out, to put shoes away so that laces aren't removed, to lock up the shampoo after washing hair, to check always that doors and windows are secure and so on. But none of this is too burdensome really, and in many cases he is a reason to encourage good habits.

It is true too they have to make allowances for Gabriel, to learn patience and tolerance, but that does them no harm either; nor that they have had to be more independent than other children of the same age or more responsible. At times of course they do feel annoyed if he interferes with their things or they are irritated by his obsessions and occasionally hit out at him as they would at any brother. These are natural and normal reactions and shouldn't be denied; he can't help his behaviour, but sometimes neither can they. Nor should we forget here that plenty of children have trouble – sometimes lifelong difficulties – with their so-called normal brothers and sisters.

In the end children are very adaptable, and without trying to belittle the difficulties I think most of them come to accept and love their handicapped sibling. What is more many are fiercely loyal to a disabled member of the family and feel they have benefited from their experiences as much as they may have lost out.

Sunday 29 May

We collected Gabriel from The Haven at midday.

We found him twirling a hair ribbon in a corner of the lounge. A couple of other residents were sprawled in front of, though paying no attention to, a huge TV screen (the colour control set at its most lurid) while a young woman, a member of staff, was mopping up a spill on the dingy carpet leaving a faint odour of disinfectant to mingle with the more enticing one of roast potatoes wafting from the kitchen.

He jumped up eagerly when he saw us and took us straight to the front door, anxious to get home as soon as possible; his bag was ready packed so it was only necessary to put on his shoes. Impatiently he waited while someone went to find them (he had apparently put one of them down the lavatory in a moment of temper and it was being dried out) and Neil put the shoes on him while I checked nothing was missing from his bag – every item has to be named and listed each time he visits, right down to his toothbrush. Lisa, who was in charge, handed over Gabriel's medication and told us about his week. We were relieved to hear there had been no big dramas, just the usual litany of fits, late nights, good days, bad days, constipation and an occasional obstinacy over his tablets. She thought he'd missed us, once or twice appearing upset that the taxi was bringing him back to The Haven rather than home. It had all been entered in the book, which was in his bag. Overall he'd had a good stay, had even enjoyed an outing to a local wildlife park and stroked a goat.

As Lisa was telling us this one of the other clients, a teenage girl, lurched down the corridor and, taking Neil's hand in a vice-like grip, thrust her face in his and began to pour out a convoluted rigmarole about 'lollies'. The words were barely intelligible (she seemed to have some cerebral palsy) as she struggled and strained in the effort to speak, plucking at his sleeve urgently. How strong her desire was to communicate; the words came tumbling out: 'lolly… minibus… red… K-K-Kev…'

'Yes, that's right, Cathy,' interrupted one of the care workers. 'We went out this morning and you had a red lolly, didn't you?' 'Yes! yes!' excitedly, 'And K-' 'And Kevin dropped his. Now let go of Gabriel's daddy's hand. Come on, let go now,' and still chattering about lollies Cathy was prised away as Gabriel, shoes now on and unwilling to delay a minute longer, leapt to his feet and made for the door. Lisa undid the various locking devices and he threw down his ribbon (*that* belongs at The Haven), snatched a tendril of the jasmine by the porch for the journey home and scrambled into the car. He demolished a gigantic meal when we got back then, happy to be reunited with the twirlers he hadn't seen for a week, spent the rest of the day wandering contentedly around the house and garden.

Feeling revitalised and positive after our trip to the Dales, even the prospect of Gabriel being home for the week ahead (half-term again) didn't daunt me. As I switched back into care mode I vowed I would try harder to keep calm. I would make more of an effort to respect and understand my son. (Easy to do this on a good day, but will it all go flying out of the window as soon as he has a 'wobbly' or snatches some of my chips? Almost certainly.)

But although he exasperates me, Gabriel also intrigues me. What is it with the twirling and fiddling? Why does he do it so relentlessly? Does he do it to blot out unwanted impressions, words he can make no sense of, sights that threaten or disturb? Is he creating a 'dream screen' in which he can lose himself?

The many repetitive behaviours in which autistic children and adults take pleasure seem to fulfil several functions; their tappings and spinnings, flickings and turnings appear to provide both security and release. On the one hand the behaviour is a way of maintaining sameness, a mechanism to cope with threatening changes; on the other hand it acts as a discharge when outer circumstances or inner turmoils are too difficult to deal with – we know the more upset Gabriel is, the more frenetically he twirls. Maybe it's like smoking a cigarette – calming during times of pressure, at other times a pleasure, and at others an irresistible addiction. Or, and one might overlook such a mundane explanation, is it, like smoking, often simply a way of coping with the tedium and boredom of everyday existence?

Looked at like this the twirling is perfectly understandable and, like some other behaviours, is not far removed from a lot of so-called normal behaviour. Bored, we watch junk TV; Gabriel watches spinning J-cloths. Stressed or in emotional pain, we give ourselves lung cancer or cirrhosis of the liver; he bangs his head against a wall or pinches himself until he draws blood. Many normal people also mutilate themselves when nervous by, say, chewing the inside of their lips or nail biting, yet if Gabriel injures himself when overload threatens it is regarded as abnormal.

Similarly, although a resistance to change and an insistence on routine is a typical feature of autism, how many of us are not ruled by habit? We like to sit in the same place at the table, eat the same food, take the same route to the station and read the same paper. We even make the same remarks to the same people, if we're not careful. We are put out if the newsagent has sold out of our favourite paper, upset over something as insignificant as losing a shirt button and stressed if our routine is disrupted. If we don't have a temper tantrum in the circumstances it is because we know the rules. We have absorbed the knowledge of what is acceptable or not and have some perspective on the situation; that knowledge and vantage point is denied to the person suffering from autism.

Wednesday 1 June

Amazing! While I was upstairs Gabriel prepared himself some Weetabix. Put it in the dish, poured on the milk, covered it liberally with sugar (of course) and – this is the most impressive bit – made hardly any mess. Though we do encourage him to do things for himself, we obviously do far too much for him. It's the easy option. It's too much trouble to get him to do things for himself. He's so slow and messy. The taxi is waiting – and so on. And we've got lazy.

Thursday 2 June

All smiles today – especially when he stripped off and ran into the garden. Another instance of not understanding the rules. In this case, where and when it's all right to be naked – or rather, not all right.

Saturday 4 June

We took Gabriel to buy some new shoes this morning.

This of course would be a simple undertaking with a normal child, even a pleasant little outing, but it is a task that requires a strategy with Gabriel. Buying new clothes is straightforward enough; since many of the children are not able to cope with zips and buttons the school advises us sensibly to stick to garments which are easy to take on and off (too easy to take off, one is sometimes tempted to think). T-shirts, sweatshirts and elasticated tracksuit bottoms are ideal – cheap, practical and not out of place anywhere Gabriel is likely to be. Their chief advantage so far as I am concerned is that they can be bought without having to try them on. Not so with shoes.

We cannot go from shop to shop waiting to be served and trying on various pairs. We'll be lucky if we manage to get a single pair on

Gabriel who hates to have his clothing interfered with once he is dressed for the day, and whose patience will have reached its limit in about three minutes.

But forewarned is forearmed. I had already checked out the selection in the local shoe shop. Did they have anything with a velcro fastening in a size 8? To my surprise they had just the thing, some sturdy casuals that even his brothers would wear – were it not for the velcro. I explained briefly about Gabriel – learning difficulties, very impatient, and so on – and arranged to bring him in early this morning, before the shop was busy. The assistant promised to be ready for us.

We had to warn Gabriel too. At least we told him several times where we were going and hoped something penetrated. He looks suspicious as we enter the shop, is relucant to take off his own shoes and puts them back on again twice before Neil manages to get the new ones on. We all try to ascertain they are the right size in the few seconds before he kicks them off, determinedly replaces his old ones on the wrong feet and jumps up ready to go. Still, we've had time to be sure they're big enough and I pay while Neil grabs him to correct the ones he's wearing as Gabriel breaks into some angry chest thumping. Quickly now, out of the shop and home. Mission accomplished.

With one exception, Gabriel expresses no preferences or desires regarding his clothes. He never adjusts them according to the temperature, never discards a sweater if it becomes hot or searches for one if it turns cold. Hot, cold, wet, dirty, old or new, he doesn't care or seem to notice – but his coat is different. He has an umbilical attachment to his coat, would like to keep it on at all times, even indoors by a blazing fire. Donna Williams was also very attached to her coat. In fact she writes that she almost lived in her duffle coat for eight years, and even referred to it as her 'mobile home'. Her coat gave her a feeling of security – and I guess Gabriel's does the same.

Sunday 5 June

Neil's brother is here for a couple of days and he offers to take Gabriel for a walk along the towpath. Living next to a canal, the towpath, with its absence of traffic, offers an ideal walk and brother-in-law sets off nonchalantly with Gabriel bounding ahead. Ten minutes later they are back, brother-in-law looking sheepish and Gabriel dripping from head to toe. 'I couldn't stop him. He just ran on then turned, looked me right in the eye, as if to say "What are you going to do about this then?" – and stepped into the canal.' New shoes and all.

Cousin Mary, Victor of Aveyron and Peter the Wild Boy

Tuesday 7 June

I have been to visit Cousin Mary – as my father always called her – Mary being the daughter of Auntie Maggie, his mother's sister.

Maggie had been a brilliant scholar at Oxford where, after gaining a Double First in 'Greats' – classics and philosophy – she later became a don. There she met her husband, also a scholar and don at the university. Marriage came late for both of them – she was by then in her early forties and he almost sixty – but soon after in 1919, Mary, their only child was born. She was, according to my father, 'a mongol'.

Fortunately for Mary her parents loved her and were sufficiently well-off to be able to engage nurses and governesses to look after and educate their daughter. Occasionally there were visits from her only cousins, my father and his sister, but these were rare and anyway there was an age gap of at least ten years between them.

Mary was 12 when tragedy struck and her mother died suddenly in a cycling accident. Her father, now 70, struggled to keep her at home, but soon the inevitable happened and Mary was moved to a house run by nuns for the 'feeble minded'. Before her father died he arranged for a trust to be set up to manage his daughter's affairs and welfare, my father being one of the trustees, and it was only with regard to this that I had heard an occasional reference to her. Once, I remember, the fact that she had lived so long was remarked on, this apparently being unexpected. Unexpected too was the death of my father before his cousin, my aunt taking his place as trustee. More recently still one of her daughters – my first cousin – decided to look up this mysterious relative whom none of us of the younger generation had ever seen.

To our astonishment her first comment after meeting Mary was that, 'She's not a mongol at all!' What was more, my cousin went on to say, one of the carers at the home had given it as her opinion that she could be autistic. (This was curious. Did my father not know the difference between people with Down's syndrome and those with other disabilities? Or did he use the word 'mongol' to mean 'mentally handicapped'? Since he was an Oxford graduate himself and a social worker and Mary was his cousin, one would not have expected such ignorance. Or was this an example of just how much ignorance existed – and still exists – about those with a mental handicap, even among so-called educated people. Until we had Gabriel I would have had to include myself among them.)

This news interested me greatly. It is not known whether there is a hereditary factor in the causes of autism, though studies of identical twins where both suffer from autism and a higher incidence of autism among siblings are providing strong evidence that the condition may have a genetic basis. Partly for this reason, I wanted to visit Mary myself. Yesterday therefore I set off to meet her with a present of a colouring book and some felt pens in my bag. Due to a period of unmanageable behaviour many years ago she had been transferred from the care of the nuns to her present home where she now lived with about ten other residents.

The home had originally been a large family house so it was small enough to be as friendly and homely as it is possible for such places to be – and Mary was expecting me. Now aged 75 and having been in care for nearly 60 years her visitors are very few and far between and she was waiting eagerly. 'Have you brought me anything?' she asked as soon as we met, eyes riveted to my bag, and then accepted my offering dismissively, while I was struck by how young and spritely she appeared for her age – doubtless the result of a lifetime without cares or responsibility.

The usual smell of disinfectant and overcooked cauliflower lingered in the hall and corridors as she led me to her room and I found the dull neutral colours and wipe-clean surfaces and materials faintly depressing. Surely these places could be made more attractive?

The room is not large – it seems quite small in fact due to all the 'clutter' Mary has amassed. The shelves by her bed are spilling over with children's story books, colouring books and dot-to-dot books – no wonder she wasn't impressed by another one – and every available surface is piled high with soft cuddly toys. I notice there is a harmonium in the corner and am told Mary used to play a simple tune on it occasionally, but now it is almost buried under a heap of teddies and bunnies, all spotless and apparently brand new. On another shelf there is a faded photograph of her parents in a frame and once she says unprompted: 'I used to have a daddy, didn't I?'

We look at her books and she writes her name for me in a large childlike hand – the full extent of her writing skills – but otherwise she seems content to pass the time just sitting, rocking gently and now and then repeating a remark or request. 'You brought me a present, didn't you? Bring a teddy next time.' There is no to and fro in our exchanges and she shows no curiosity towards me. When I ask her about her cousins – my father and my aunt – she has no idea who I am talking about. She puts the television on but doesn't look at it and soon turns it off. Apparently bored, she lets me know it's time I went. I say goodbye. 'Goodbye,' says Mary, 'bring me a toy next time.' I make a note of her birthday and a reminder to send her one and then I leave, still wondering if she suffers from autism (I'm inclined to think she might but of course am not qualified to say) and if there exists a tenuous but significant link between Gabriel and his grandfather's first cousin.

Of course whether Cousin Mary suffered from autism or not, the fact is that it was only in the 1940s that the condition was recognised and named. Yet it seems likely that there have always been individuals with autism and indeed there exist descriptions of people with characteristics typical of the disorder and recognisable to us today. One of the most famous accounts is of a boy known as the Wild Boy

of Aveyron, a fascinating portrait full of familiar details and sim-
ilarities with our own Wild Boy.

On 8 January 1800, in the Department of Aveyron in France, a
naked boy aged about twelve walked into a villager's house and soon
became the talk of the country. His existence was already known
locally. Peasants had sometimes spotted him swimming and drinking
in streams, climbing trees, running swiftly on all fours and searching
for and eating roots and acorns; occasionally he gave deep cries or
laughed up at the sky.

The boy had in fact been caught twice before – not without a
struggle – but each time had regained his liberty shortly after. He had
also entered farms and accepted food – though it appeared he ate
nothing but potatoes or nuts – before disappearing once more. This
time however he again fell captive and from that moment on became
an object of study and debate, remaining so until the present day, the
subject of several books and a film *L'Enfant Sauvage*.

Although the boy was simply assumed by some to be an abandoned imbecile, others disagreed and saw his capture as a unique
opportunity to study a human being whose formative years had been
spent in isolation, untouched and untainted by society. How would
he develop? Could more be discovered about the process of learning
and man's socialisation? What about language? Here was a chance to
observe the effects of society and education on a primitive and
undeveloped being. Descriptions and eyewitness accounts from the
time of his capture survive, as well as an account by the young
physician to whose care he was entrusted. They make fascinating
reading. Victor, as he was named by Itard the physician, is now
considered by many to have been autistic.

The first account of the Wild Boy was written by the government
commissioner for the village where he had been caught, who hurried
to see this child everyone was talking about and said was a wild beast:

> I found him seated in front of a fire that appeared to give him
> great pleasure but he was disquieted from time to time, which I
> attributed to the large gathering of people around him. I looked
> at him for some time without saying a word; then I spoke to him;

and it didn't take long to realise he was mute. When I noticed that he gave no response to the various questions that I put to him, both loudly and softly, I concluded that he was deaf.

The commissioner persuaded Victor to return with him to his home:

Once back at the house I thought he would be hungry, and I saw to it that he got something to eat. On the way back, people had tried to persuade me that the boy lived off roots and other raw vegetables. In order to confirm this or to learn his tastes, I had a large earthen plate prepared, with raw and cooked meat, rye and wheat bread, apples, pears, grapes, walnuts, chestnuts, acorns, potatoes, parsnip roots, and an orange. He confidently took the potatoes first and threw them into the middle of the fire to cook. He seized each of the other foods in turn, smelled them and rejected them. I told my servant to get more potatoes and he rejoiced in seeing them; he took them in his two hands and threw them into the fire. A moment later he reached his right hand into the coals and took out and ate the potatoes, while they were still burning hot. There was no way to make him wait until they had cooled off a bit; he burned himself, and expressed his pain by loud and inarticulate sounds, which were however not plaintive. When he became thirsty, he looked left and right; spotting a pitcher, without making the least sign he took my hand in his and led me to it; then he struck the pitcher with his left hand, thus asking me for something to drink. He was brought wine, which he rejected, showing great impatience with my delay in giving him water.

This frugal lunch finished, he got up and ran through the door; despite my cries, he continued to flee so that I had a hard time catching him. I led him back without his making any sign of pleasure or displeasure. He had already interested me greatly as a hapless child; I began to have other feelings, those of surprise and curiosity. His refusal of bread and meat, his preference for potatoes, the sort of agreeable sensation he seemed to get from looking at an acorn that had been given to him and that he held in his hand longer than any other object, his air of satisfaction that nothing could trouble – except occasionally, although he was utterly destitute, the realisation that he was deprived of the open air – led me to conclude that this boy had lived in the woods since his early childhood, a stranger to social needs and practices.

This initial description has so many echoes of our son's behaviour I couldn't help but be struck by it. The boy was mute and the writer concluded he was deaf – as I have already said many people assumed Gabriel was deaf also. He apparently preferred raw to cooked food and smelled everything he was offered. Gabriel also, besides enjoying raw foods such as salads, often takes raw meat, potatoes or uncooked dough (a particular favourite). He too always smells any unfamiliar food and like Victor is extremely impatient and will eat his food before it has cooled. Victor 'expressed his pain by loud inarticulate sounds, which were however not plaintive', similarly Gabriel confines himself to a few yelps of complaint when hurt, appearing relatively insensitive to pain. When Victor wanted water he took the writer's hand to the pitcher, just as Gabriel and many autistic people make their needs known. The Wild Boy's propensity to 'flee' at great speed at the least opportunity is of course another reminder of our own wild boy, while Victor's preoccupation with an acorn and 'the agreeable sensation he seemed to derive from holding it and looking at it' echoes Gabriel's interest in odd objects – a teapot lid or the tin of talcum powder can occupy him for hours.

In a letter written the following day another observer finds it difficult to understand how a naked child could have withstood the rigours of the preceding, exceptionally cold winter. The boy was a mystery. Not only was nothing known about him and he could tell of nothing himself but there was 'something extraordinary in his behaviour, which makes him seem close to the state of wild animals'. (Perhaps here it might be said that stories of 'wolf' children – children supposedly brought up by animals and found living wild, which are reported from time to time, could also be accounts of autistic children. Such children could easily become lost, especially in a period of great upheaval or, because of the difficulties they present, might be abandoned by their families.)

Gabriel's behaviour is often feral too. Victor drank from streams; on a walk Gabriel will scoop a handful of water from a puddle or bend and drink from the canal (he has a cast-iron stomach), while at home he prefers to sip water directly from the tap – like a hamster, observed his brother – rather from cup or glass. Both prefer to be naked. For propriety's sake Victor was clothed in a loose-fitting garment which however 'annoyed him greatly'. Gabriel, although accustomed to wearing clothes, still has no sense of propriety and has often run into the garden or street with no clothes on. Once he undressed in the car and got out by the sunroof while I was paying for petrol. Another animal-like habit common to both is sleeping and sitting on the ground. Though we feel there is no good reason to restrict Gabriel's freedom in this matter what surprises us is his disregard for comfort – he often chooses to lie in the coldest, draughtiest spots (this being due perhaps to an insensitivity to temperature). 'Fleeing' too could be seen as feral, though in Victor's case seemed even more so as he sometimes ran on all fours, or so they said, adding: 'nothing can console him from the loss of his freedom' – a sentiment that must be shared by many a caged animal.

In August 1800 the Wild Boy arrived in Paris, there to be observed and studied by excited scientists, philosophers and other great men. They would encounter

> a child cut off from all of society and all intellectual commun-
> ication, a child to whom no one had even spoken and who
> would be scrutinised down to the slightest movements he might
> make to express his first sensations, his first ideas, his first
> thoughts – if indeed one can think without fixed and con-
> ventional signs.

What the author of this article, written a day or two after Victor's arrival there, found most astonishing was the fact that after six months living among people, provided with all his needs and given every care the boy had not 'taken a single step toward civilisation and is today as far from our customs and habits as he was on the first day he was found'.

Equally baffling was the boy's continued mutism – and Gabriel's and many others suffering from autism. How often have we wondered if it is a question of can't talk or won't talk. How often when we have explained that he doesn't talk have we been asked,

'What, not a single word?'

'Not one.'

'But he makes noises or signs that mean something?'

'Not really, nothing but inarticulate sounds, and those not in any effort to communicate but only expressing pain or pleasure.' (Now that we have a dog I have thought more than once that the dog makes more effort than Gabriel does to communicate when he looks into my eyes and deep, longing sounds come from his chest.)

'But he understands what you say?' they continue.

'Very little.'

For many years it appeared he understood nothing at all. Not a word. Not his name, yes, no, nothing. I remember Neil's excitement when I came home after an evening out: 'I'm sure he understands "bed"! He went to the bathroom and got undressed tonight when I said it was time for bed.' This was a breakthrough – he was 4 years and 8 months old and it was his first indication he'd understood a word.

On the other hand some people who were familiar with Gabriel sometimes half-joked: 'He understands every word you say – he's just having you on.' And from time to time we would unexpectedly see that he did sometimes take in more than we gave him credit for.

'But will he talk eventually?' they persist. 'What do they say?' 'They' being the experts. Well, it was true one oracle had told us 'We don't give up until they reach 21', and there are instances of previously mute children astonishing everyone around them and suddenly bringing forth a sentence from out of the blue. Some others although not previously mute become much more articulate. Still others echo interminably, but Gabriel seems to have a definite *disinclination* to communicate. He knows the sign for 'please' but would much rather not use it. He'd prefer us to understand him from the flicker of an eyelash or the twitch of a cheek muscle, anything but look us in the eyes and communicate.

To continue with Victor we hear:

> His desires do not exceed his physical needs. The only blessings
> he knows in the universe are nourishment, rest, and independ-
> ence [liberty] ... His affections are as limited as his knowledge;
> he loves no one; he is attached to no one; and if he shows some
> preference for his caretaker, it is an expression of need and not
> the sentiment of gratitude; he follows the man because the latter
> is concerned with satisfying his needs and satiating his appetites.

If I were to describe Gabriel I couldn't have put it better. How limited
his desires are, how indifferent he is to us! Like Victor: 'When kissed,
he does not notice whether it is a man or a woman and, to put it
better, he does not care about it at all.' Also like Victor: 'If he is
thwarted, he loses his temper, becomes agitated, prances with rage,
strikes his head, bites, nips, scratches, weeps and cries out.'

For both of them food is a motivator and in Gabriel brings out
signs of intelligence not usually evident. The other Wild Boy also 'is
much inclined to theft, and quite adroit at stealing; when eating at the
table he takes everything that he wants from his neighbours, quickly
and stealthily, *even though he has those foods already*' [my italics]. Is this
another feral characteristic? It is certainly an irrepressible habit of our
own wild boy.

Victor's odd behaviour was put down to his having lived in the
wild. He had had to fend for himself to survive and at the same time
had had no contact with people and was therefore naturally totally
unsocialised. Little wonder he stole food or ran away at a gallop at the
least opportunity. He was said to detest 'children of his own age,
running away from them. This aversion comes originally, perhaps,
from his having been pursued when living in the forests.' It was also
remarked: 'He likes solitude a great deal; crowds irritate him and
make him uncomfortable and temperamental.' But as with Gabriel,
this was more probably to do with a difficulty in relating to others
than an upbringing in isolation.

Whatever the reason, here was a child who could not speak, who
behaved like an animal and whose entire existence was occupied
with his basic needs. This was the young man they hoped to study

and educate and, as Itard wrote, 'many believed that the education of this individual would be a matter of a few months, and that he would soon recount the most interesting stories concerning his earlier life'.

There were those however who felt sure that the boy was ineducable; that his behaviour was due more to his 'highly circumscribed mental faculties' than to a life in the forest. This was certainly the opinion of Pinel, an authority of the day on mental disease. Itard though remained optimistic. He felt that it was the extraordinary circumstances of Victor's former life that had affected his attention and intellectual faculties. For this reason he decided the boy must first be settled and habituated to 'normal' life (after all his capture and subsequent events must have been quite traumatic for him) and this life must be made more attractive to him before his instruction could begin. To this end Itard set about stimulating his senses and taking him out and about. He took Victor out to dine and there also remains an amusing account of a visit to Madame Récamier's salon. Here the most elevated and cultivated society of the day met and many important guests were present:

> Madame Récamier seated him at her side, thinking perhaps that the same beauty that had captivated civilised man would receive the same homage from this child of nature ... too occupied with the abundant things to eat, which he devoured with startling greed as soon as his plate was filled, the young savage hardly heeded the beautiful eyes whose attention he himself had attracted. When dessert was served and he had adroitly filled his pockets with all the delicacies that he could filch, he calmly left the table.

When a noise came from the garden Itard, followed by the other guests, went to investigate and they soon saw the fugitive:

> running across the lawn with the speed of a rabbit. To give himself more freedom of movement, he had stripped to his undershirt. Reaching the main avenue of the park, which was bordered by huge chestnut trees, he tore his last garment in two, as if it were simply made of gauze; then climbing the nearest tree

with the ease of a squirrel, he perched in the middle of the branches.

The women, motivated as much by distaste as by respect for decorum, kept to the rear while the men set about recapturing the child of the woods.

The boy ignored all entreaties to descend and

> leapt from branch to branch and from tree to tree, until there were neither trees nor branches in front of him and he reached the end of the avenue. The gardener then had the idea of showing him a basket full of peaches and, nature ceding to this argument, the runaway came down from the tree and let himself be captured. He was clothed as best one could with a little robe belonging to the gardener's niece. In this outfit he was bundled into the carriage that had brought him and he left, leaving the guests at Clichy-la-Garenne to draw a sweeping and useful comparison between the perfection of civilised life and the distressing picture of nature untamed, which this scene so strikingly contrasted.

From this account Victor still appears to have made little progress but, according to Itard, the boy did become increasingly socialised and also developed deep affection not only for his guardian but also for Itard himself who now set about teaching the boy to speak. One problem was that Victor, like Gabriel, was quite capable of making his basic needs known. 'It's quite clear what he wants' people always say when they observe Gabriel, and so it was with the *Enfant Sauvage*, though Victor actually shows far more patience and civility than our boy:

> If he is in town dining with me, he addresses all his requests to the person who does the honours of the table; it is always to her that he turns to be served. If she pretends not to hear him, he puts his plate next to the particular dish he wants and devours it with his eyes. If that produces no result, he takes a fork and strikes the edge of his plate two or three times. If she still neglects him, then he knows no bounds; he plunges a spoon or even his hand into the dish and in the twinkling of an eye

empties it all onto his own plate. He is scarcely less expressive in his way of showing his emotions, above all impatience and boredom. A number of people visiting him out of curiosity know how, with more natural frankness than politeness, he dismisses them when fatigued by the length of their visits; he offers to each of them, quite deliberately, their cane, gloves, and hat, and pushes them gently toward the door, which he slams shut behind them.

Exactly.

Obviously Victor's education presented a daunting task and it is to Itard's great credit that he eventually succeeded in teaching him to write some rudimentary sentences. It was a long and laborious task – 'the most powerful methods are used to obtain the smallest effects', but it is difficult to know how much of what he learned to write he understood. Although, according to Itard, Victor manifested feelings of affection and remorse and responded to praise, although in Itard's opinion the boy was aware of the care taken of him and sensitive to the pleasure of doing things well, he never lost his longing for the freedom of the open country nor developed a taste for the pleasures of social life. Most disappointingly of all, Victor never gratified his teacher by learning to speak. After four years the Wild Boy of Aveyron's education was abandoned and he was allowed to pass the rest of his days with his guardian Madame Guérin until, in 1828, aged about 40 and still 'fearful and half-wild,' he died, as much of a mystery as the day he had been found.

Victor was not the only *enfant sauvage* to have made his mark; by great coincidence a character known as Peter the Wild Boy spent some sixty years in the neighbouring parish in which we live. He too probably suffered from autism.

Peter's story began near Hamelin in Germany in 1725 when a farmer found him, near naked and aged about 12, in one of his fields. Like Victor he resisted capture but was finally enticed with some apples and then placed in a local hospital. Although the ragged remnants of a shirt hung round his neck no one knew where he came from or how long he had been living wild. (We have often mused on how Gabriel would make out if he got lost. Unlikely perhaps in the urban area we now inhabit – he'd probably be picked up for shoplifting the first day, if his strange behaviour or lack of road sense had not already alerted someone. But what if he found himself in the wilds of Scotland, say? Would he, like Victor and Peter, find roots and berries and shelter? I have the feeling he'd probably survive.)

Peter, it was reported, had no coherent speech, disliked wearing clothes, could climb 'like a squirrel' and liked to rest 'animal fashion on his knees and elbows'. (Strangely this is a characteristic position of Gabriel's and one that he always adopts when opening his bowels. It has long mystified us.) As with Victor enormous interest in this phenomenal young man was taken by the wise and great of the time, including 'royalty, novelists, pamphleteers, journalists, moralists and scientists'. Daniel Defoe wrote an account of his life and even long after his death Charles Dickens mentioned him in his books. (The mentally handicapped interested him and according to an article in *Communication* his character Barnaby Rudge 'is the first autistic hero in English literature'.)

Such was Peter's fame that George I, visiting Germany shortly after the boy's capture, heard of him and ordered the boy to be brought to him. Peter was apparently unimpressed by the King or the royal table; he would accept none of the delicacies he was offered until finally tempted with raw meat which he ate greedily. When the King returned to England he brought Peter with him. However, the Court soon tired of its 'unusual pet' and, as a memorial tablet in the local church tells us, since he had proved 'incapable of speaking or of receiving instruction, a comfortable provision was made for him by her Majesty at a farmhouse in this Parish, where he continued to live to the end of his inoffensive life'. The farmer was paid an annual allowance from the crown of £35 for the boy's upkeep.

Peter liked to wander. 'Don't any of your children run away?' I asked some of the other mothers – it being a constant concern of ours. Though not all parents had this worry it was not uncommon and I heard how one child had twice taken the train to London and been found drifting around King's Cross station, while another young man had run off one night and managed to break into a small supermarket where he was found several hours later raiding the biscuit shelves. Peter's surroundings and the times he lived in presumably made it possible for him to roam unhindered. According to a report in 1751 he had once even reached Norwich some 150 miles away, where he had been imprisoned as a vagrant and been reluctant to leave the prison when it caught fire, enjoying the spectacle so much.

A simple solution to this problem was soon arrived at. From then on Peter wore a heavy leather collar with a brass rim inscribed with the words 'Peter the Wild Man from Hanover' and instructions that whoever would return him to the farmer who cared for him would be paid for their trouble. (An article in the NAS magazine discusses a modern solution to this roaming tendency, the author having devised

The grave of Peter the Wild Boy

an electronic tracking device where the autistic person wears a watch-sized transmitter and the carer has a small receiver. Alarm mode alerts him if the child strays out of range; search mode helps to find him.) The collar is preserved at the local public school together with a petition from the farmer to the King for a larger allowance to cover expenses incurred by Peter's wanderings.

Throughout his life Peter enjoyed a certain notoriety. His effigy appeared in a waxworks in the Strand in 1774 and he was sought out by numerous visitors who paid to see him sing and dance, which apparently he was happy to do. There were many stories written about him but one in particular reminded me of Gabriel. He occasionally helped the farmer and one day was filling a dung cart with his master who left him alone to finish the task. Peter had soon filled the cart, and then in order to keep working had proceeded to empty it! At mealtimes we encourage Gabriel to help clear the table and he often takes the dishes out to the kitchen as instructed, but then not knowing what to do with them carries them back to the table.

At last, after almost sixty years of an 'inoffensive' life Peter died in 1785, aged about 72. He was buried in the local churchyard and a simple stone is inscribed with the date and the name he was always known by – Peter the Wild Boy.

12

Autism

What is it? What causes it?
What can be done about it?

I have covered Victor's and Peter's stories in some detail because they so resemble Gabriel. Long before we had ever heard of either of them we ourselves had often described him as wild because of his unsocialised and feral behaviour. Yet put simply autism or Autistic Spectrum Disorder (ASD), as its new name implies, covers a wide range of ability extending from children and adults such as Gabriel to those who have average or above average intelligence, verbal and non-verbal skills. People included in this part of the spectrum are mostly said to have Asperger's syndrome. There are also the children and adults with exceptional skills or remarkable talents – able to play a piece of music after one hearing, to compose, draw prodigiously or perform amazing calculations, even though often being of low ability in other areas. These people are sometimes referred to as 'idiots savants' or wise fools. Lately, as more and more is becoming known of the disorder, it seems the wider the boundary extends, including now people apparently functioning well in all aspects of their lives (having jobs, partners, families, etc.) yet who suffer from many characteristic autistic traits, albeit in diluted form. What then, one might think, could Gabriel possibly have in common with these more able individuals?

ASD is a developmental disability affecting over 500,000 people in the UK according to the latest figures. It affects the way a person communicates and relates to others; imagination is also affected. Difficulties in these areas vary widely but are nonetheless present in all people with autism, despite differences in intelligence and ability. I have already mentioned many features associated with autism. Some of them, however, although common, are not always present. It is the overall picture that is important: problems with social interaction, communication and imagination, allied with a repetitive pattern of activities. Where these might be very apparent in some, in others they are not so easily recognised. Children suffering from Asperger's syndrome, for example, are often not diagnosed until their teens or later.

The apparent aloofness and indifference to other people is perhaps one of the most well-known characteristics. All people with ASD have difficulty relating to and interacting with others (particularly other children). One mother wrote that from babyhood her son who suffered from Asperger's syndrome regarded other children 'as a different species'. Although some children are less aloof and many become more sociable with age, they continue to relate inappropriately. Even the more able ones tend to behave towards others in an unnaturally formal, stilted way and their peers find them odd and self-obsessed. They seem to have little understanding of how others think and feel: 'the emotion circuit's not hooked up' according to one sufferer. Sadly, although they might desperately wish it, they find it very difficult to make friends. Social niceties need to be learned; what one says or doesn't say in a given situation, and naturally the pitfalls are legion. One young man anxious to make the acquaintance of a pretty girl had been taught that in dealings with the opposite sex compliments on dress or appearance were much appreciated. He was very pleased to recount after a date that he hadn't forgotten this piece of advice – he had told the girl how beautifully her dress set off the colour of her gums.

Problems with language and communication affect all people with autism. Plainly, the choice of *Communication* as the title of the National Autistic Society's magazine was made to draw attention to this most obvious disability – as well as to act as a forum for others to voice their thoughts, feelings and findings on autism. A substantial minority, like Gabriel, remain mute all their lives and others only develop a limited repertoire of words and phrases which are often parrotted endlessly and inappropriately. On the other hand the speech and language of some develop considerably, while those with Asperger's syndrome usually have no delay in either.

Although not so obvious, even those with wide vocabularies have problems of communication. They do not appreciate its social uses and pleasures and tend to speak *at* others rather than *with* them, or to talk obsessively on their favourite topics. Language is often understood very literally. One boy on being told he could wear a daffodil as it was St David's day said he'd rather wear a jumper as usual. Common expressions such as 'give someone a hand' or 'to nearly die laughing' can be mystifying, or worse quite terrifying; to the person with ASD it appears that non-autistic people often speak in riddles. (Autistic people do not tell lies either.) But not only are there difficulties with actual words, people with autism have little comprehension of body language, gesture, facial expression or tone of voice and those who have no speech do not use signs or gestures to communicate, though they might eventually learn some signs. (Although Gabriel has learned to sign 'please' we have never managed to teach him to point – something young babies do naturally and with enthusiasm.)

Besides these impairments the child with autism also suffers from an impairment of the imagination; as, for example, in an inability to play imaginatively with toys or in pretend games. Perhaps the 'literalness' of their minds explains why they do not engage in symbolic play. For them a pile of wooden bricks is *not* a house, and mud in a toy saucepan is *not* a pudding. Bricks or cars are arranged in long straight lines, or the child spends hours spinning the wheels of his toy cars rather than pushing them along to 'vroom, vroom' noises. This lack of pretend play with objects extends to characters. In normal play a child sits in a cardboard box and pretends he is driving a train and his playmate is a passenger. To play the game each child has to put himself in the place of another. When he plays doctors and nurses or cowboys and indians he has already absorbed the knowledge and observed that other people behave in certain ways and have their own thoughts and feelings. People with autism seem unable to do this and if, as occasionally happens, they do act out a character it is over and over in the same way with the same words and actions. Similarly, the same stories are listened to and the same videos watched time after time, with little understanding. For the more intelligent ones there is an inability to understand fiction. 'I could read them all right,' wrote Donna Williams of novels 'but I was unable to pick up what the book was about.' Temple Grandin, another 'high functioning' person with ASD, confessed to being 'bewildered' by Romeo and Juliet – she 'never knew what they were up to'.

Finally they all indulge in repetitive stereotyped activities and the variations here are endless and idiosyncratic: from flicking fingers or spinning objects to tapping, rocking and jumping; from an obsession with a particular sound to compulsively collecting buttons, pieces of cloth, milk bottle tops, pebbles, etc; from lengthy routines and rituals to an insistence on and fascination with certain topics – anything from burglar alarms to washing machines, telephone directories to World War I. There is often an insistence on 'sameness'. Chairs must always be in the same position, toilet paper must always be pink, getting ready for school must be done in a precise and undeviating order. (Itard noted that Victor had a definite liking for order and many a time I have placed an extra chair at the table for a guest only to find it removed and returned to its customary home as soon as I turned my back. 'He's very tidy,' said one of Gabriel's teachers, 'even replacing the petals on the flowers on my desk when they start to fall at the end of the week.')

Physically although the children do not look different (and have a normal life expectancy unless suffering some other disability such as epilepsy) they often move awkwardly (on tiptoes or with head bent over) or have odd posture (hands hanging limply), those with Asperger's syndrome being typically clumsy. Challenging behaviour is common, making life difficult for their carers, while abnormal responses to sensory stimuli – sound, sight, pain, etc. – are often present making life bewildering to themselves.

As the autistic spectrum covers a wide range one fortunate aspect of this fact is that some of the more high functioning individuals can tell us how they experience life and themselves. Several sufferers have written of their experiences and reading these accounts has given me some insight into the way Gabriel thinks and feels. Of course I can only infer from what I have read that Gabriel experiences himself similarly. Every autistic individual differs and has his or her own character and it would be dangerous to assume too much. Nonetheless I have found it helpful to get a view from the inside looking out as it were, and many of the descriptions do seem to correlate with and explain some behaviour.

Donna Williams has written several books about her life. In *Nobody Nowhere* and *Somebody Somewhere* she describes her world and why she felt so cut off from the world outside. One of the reasons for her isolation was that she existed for much of the time in a kind of 'sensory hell' as she puts it. It seems that for the autistic person the senses can be exceptionally acute – sometimes to an almost intolerable degree.

To take hearing first, why is it that so often the children are thought to be deaf? Donna was tested for deafness on several occasions although she could speak and all the tests confirmed she could hear. The last examination however found that not only was her hearing better than average but that she could even hear some frequencies only animals normally hear. She talks about the 'painfulness of sounds' and of sounds as an 'unintelligible mass of noise'. Temple Grandin (who like Donna has written about her experience of autism: '*Emergence; Labelled Autistic*') also tells of being a victim of jumbled sound which seemed to bombard her at overwhelming volume; 'Loud noise hurt my ears.' Therese Jolliffe, another woman with autism, has written of her experiences and she lists many sounds, such as shouting and noisy vehicles, that she finds so upsetting she has to cover her ears to avoid them. (Paradoxically, some particular sounds may have a fascination. Donna loved metallic sounds, including the family's front door bell, which she rang so obsessively that her parents were driven to remove it.)

This hypersensitivity to sound and the pain it causes is sometimes too much and Temple says that she was able to shut out noise and over-stimulation when it became too intense and retreat into her own world. Donna too could shut out sound. Like Gabriel she would not so much as blink when her parents made loud noises behind her. Therese did not respond sometimes because her 'quietness was being disturbed'; she too was tested for deafness several times.

At the same time there was the problem of interpreting sound. When Donna's hearing was tested at the age of 9 it was because although she could speak she hadn't responded to being spoken to. She described herself as 'meaning deaf' explaining that: 'In terms of the effect on one's life, it largely amounts to being deaf. One is robbed not of sound but of the meaning of sound.' Therese puts it slightly differently:

> When I was very young I can remember that speech seemed to be of no more significance than any other sound. For a time speech sounds seemed just to merge into one another without making any sense, a jumble of letters, hard to reproduce, let alone understand.

It was a long time before she realised that some of the speech was directed at her and required her attention. If this was the case with people who later could write books and get degrees, then how much more confusing must language be to the Gabriels of the autistic spectrum.

When we come to sight, Therese writes: 'I find it as difficult to understand the things I see as I do in trying to understand the things I hear.' As for Donna, one of her first memories was that 'the air was full of spots. If you looked into nothingness there were spots'. She would lose herself in the spots, or stars as she sometimes called them, and wrote: 'I have since learned that they are actually air particles yet my vision was so hypersensitive that they often became a hypnotic foreground with the rest of "the world" fading away.' She loved too, and could lose herself in, the reflections of light and colour and 'tracing every patterned shape' – 'the beautiful side of autism' as she put it. But the hypersensitivity was also painful and she described being 'tortured by sharp white fluorescent light, which made reflections bounce off everything. It made the room race busily in a constant state of change'.

The main problem with sight however was looking at people – at their faces and particularly into their eyes. All these women reiterate how difficult they found – and continue to find – eye contact. Therese writes: 'People do not appreciate how unbearably difficult it is for me to look at a person. It disturbs my quietness and is terribly frightening.' For this reason she explained she tended to look at people 'when they are unaware of it', while Donna describes three ways in which she had avoided looking at people.

> One was to look straight through what was in front of me. Another was to look away at something else. The third was to stare blankly ahead with one eye and turn the other one inwards. This had the effect of blurring whatever view I had in front of me.

I recognise these stratagems in Gabriel's way of looking. I was especially struck by the last one as in a similar way he often looks ahead with one eye while directing the other upwards or outwards – a habit he developed when about a year old.

A refusal to look one in the eye is often very noticeable in people with autism, but what I hadn't realised was that, according to Therese, 'It is almost as bad having other people looking at me as it is me looking at them.' Donna writes: 'Dr M was "touching" me with his eyes. I was afraid.' Looking into the eyes is not so far from body contact – and the fear of touch.

I have already mentioned Gabriel's and other autistic people's aversion to hugs and cuddles. (I should say here that, though exceedingly common, this is not true of all sufferers of autism.) The dislike of intimate contact is an aspect of the condition that often sends a chill through the heart. What strange creatures are these who reject what most of us would consider an instinctive desire or need – the warmth and comfort of touch? Yet for autistic people like Temple, what might appear as a rejection of others is rather an oversensitivity to touch that makes physical contact disturbing and painful. 'I pulled away when people tried to hug me,' she writes, 'because being touched sent an overwhelming tidal wave of stimulation through my body... My reaction to being touched was like a wild horse flinching and pulling away.'

Donna also flinched when anyone came too close: 'He touched my hair. I pulled away. "It burns me," I explained. "All touch is pain."' Donna's aversion to touch lay not so much in physical sensitivity but: 'It was the threat of losing all sense of separateness between myself and the other person. Like being eaten up, or drowned by a tidal wave, fear of touch was the same as fear of death.'

As a child Temple *wanted* 'the comforting feeling of being held' but *avoided* it because of the effect it had on her nervous system. According to her, 'Abnormalities of the cerebellum may explain why an autistic child pulls away and stiffens when touched.' (She wonders whether 'it would be beneficial to gently stroke autistic babies when they pull away and "tame" them when they are very young.' But often parents do not know their babies are suffering from autism. That is the problem.) Because of her own 'craving' for the feeling of being held, Temple later as an adolescent built what she called her 'squeeze machine'.

This machine she developed and built after coming across a similar machine used to hold or restrain calves, which seemed to have a calming effect on them. It was a body-sized padded wooden trough with controls connected to an industrial compressor. To use the machine she lay on the bottom facing the controls and when she switched it on the sides converged, exerting a deep and comfortable pressure on her body. (Since acquiring a dog I have noticed that he usually chooses to lie pressed against something solid or he squeezes himself into a tight corner against a wall or piece of furniture – perhaps also for the comforting sensation of pressure.) Temple designed and constructed the squeeze machine herself, being very competent in that respect – as well as being an internationally recognised expert on animal behaviour and 'livestock facility design', university lecturer and business woman. She made it so she was able to control the amount and duration of the pressure.

By using the machine the over-sensitivity of her nervous system was gradually reduced and the sensation of touch and being held became first tolerable and then pleasurable. Being in the squeeze machine was and is – she still uses it many years later – both comforting and calming and what is more, Temple says, it also helps her to *feel more* for her family and friends.

Donna didn't have a squeeze machine but was determined in her own way to overcome her fear of touch or closeness. It scared her. She knew she had let people touch her in the past (this is apart from necessary touch such as by a doctor or dentist), but since she hadn't acknowledged it was her *self* who had been touched that hadn't really counted. In the same way it didn't really count if only her clothes were touched. The sleeve was not her arm.

Touch had not been received as social or emotional touch and Donna certainly didn't touch others to express feelings of attachment or pleasure. In fact she had no concept that touch was connected with these feelings; for her it was an invasion and a terror. However she gradually came to recognise and understand that in 'the' world (as opposed to in 'her' world) people enjoy and welcome contact. So with great courage she set out to acquire the feelings which she lacked; she wanted to want to touch and hug a favourite person. Donna was 27 years old when she was able to do this for the first time in her life. She had begun to learn how to feel.

When we read of the difficulties these people have to cope with, people who can reason and ask questions, then how much more confusing and frustrating must Gabriel and those like him find life. I have often thought with regard to his situation that for him 'ignorance is bliss', that he has no idea of his state. Yet he displays so much of the behaviour described by the more articulate sufferers of autism that I can't help feeling much of it must arise from the same causes.

How I wish now we had known more about autism when he was younger and I sometimes feel bad when I look back and remember how I treated him. Almost certainly he was more aware than we realised and perhaps was not so indifferent to others as we assumed. Was it the same for him as for a 17-year-old boy who wrote that when he was young: 'I used to have a lot of temper tantrums and scream and shout and bite myself and jump up and down. The hard thing was that nobody liked me and I used to feel upset about it.' Or another young man who wrote that because of his inability to communicate most people thought he was retarded and that he had no thoughts or feelings that mattered.

Was it like that for Gabriel? I hope not.

Because sometimes the signs of autism are so subtle, and since it is a developmental disability, it only becomes apparent gradually (not always though; sometimes the onset can be an inexplicable and sudden regression – perhaps the origin behind stories of change-lings). Since there is no simple test that can be used to give a positive answer to the question 'Is this child suffering from autism?' the journey from the first vague signs to the final diagnosis is often a long and tortuous one.

This is partly because it was only relatively recently (1940s) that the condition was recognised and given a name and though many professionals are more familiar with the signs of autism than, say, 20 years ago, it is still not common or easily detected. One must also not forget that with the less able ones there is a great deal of overlap with learning disabled children who are not autistic. Films such as *Rainman* (an excellent portrayal of a young man with autism), newspaper articles and documentaries on TV have greatly increased public awareness, but it remains a fact that one of the problems for parents of children with autistic disorders is getting a diagnosis. In their quest to find an answer to their initial concerns, parents have been told that they were over-anxious and neurotic, there was nothing to worry about or, conversely, that they were too aggressive and overbearing and were actually causing the problem behaviour themselves. They have been told their children were schizophrenic, psychotic or simply in need of 'a good spanking'.

The eventual diagnosis when it comes is usually received with a mixture of devastation and relief; devastation at the news that, yes there is something wrong with your child, and relief that you now have a name for it. In the words of one father: 'I can recall it frame by frame. Leaving the hospital, making a joke and then collapsing into floods of tears ... [his wife] felt a sense of relief because she felt that at last we knew what it was and could do something about it.' Inevitable questions then follow: Why does my child suffer from autism? What caused it? Can it be cured? Unfortunately there are no straightforward answers to these questions.

At first when the condition was categorised and given a name it was believed to be an emotional or psychological disorder arising from the way the children had been brought up – the 'blame the parents' theory. The prevalence of Freud's ideas for the reasons behind aberrant behaviour were a major influence at the time and the very abnormal behaviour of children with autism was ascribed to unaffectionate parents who did not relate normally to their children.

To be blamed for your child's disorder was very distressing and potentially damaging, to say the least. There are commonly feelings of guilt anyway and these ideas only added to them at a time when parents were often in a desperate – and I do not use that word lightly – situation. It did not seem to occur to anyone that the difficulty in relating on the part of the parents might have arisen *because* of the behaviour, because of the aloofness and indifference. In fact some parents almost feel they have given birth to a creature from another planet, so strange and mysteriously remote are their offspring, which seems to be how some of the children themselves experience their situation. Temple Grandin said she felt like 'an anthropologist from Mars' (in the book of that title by Oliver Sacks) and Donna Williams distinguished constantly between our world and her world. Yet another autistic author entitled her book *Through the Eyes of Aliens*.

Now, new knowledge and research have discredited this theory – though it has not entirely disappeared – and autism is considered to be a biological deficit leading to a disorder of development. As Lorna Wing writes in *The Autistic Spectrum*: 'Growing knowledge of the way the brain functions and the things that can go wrong have made it clear that the causes are physical and nothing to do with child-rearing methods.'

The case for a physical cause is made stronger by the fact that many of the children suffer other disorders such as epilepsy and learning difficulties and that boys affected far outnumber girls. It appears that there is no single cause, but more probably a variety of them. These include genetic factors (Cousin Mary in Gabriel's case?), medical conditions such as rubella, tuberose sclerosis, an encephalitis resulting from a viral infection and Fragile X syndrome.

With so many lines of investigation to pursue and given the nature of autism, it is not surprising that when we ask what can be done about it or if it can be cured there are conflicting views. However it is mostly accepted that there is, as yet, no cure for autism. This might sound bleak, yet unlike a degenerative condition which steadily gets worse, because autism is a developmental disorder the children tend rather to improve slowly as they get older. Some, generally the more able ones, improve immeasurably. Yet the autism remains. They simply become autistic adults better able to cope with their autism (and maybe in the eyes of some they are cured). Although this is also true of children like Gabriel there is less noticeable improvement among the more disabled. Yet now and again we hear of dramatic 'cures' or of another 'breakthrough'.

In dire straits we all hope for miracles. We might laugh at them when we are strong, healthy and our lives are going well, but if something befalls us from which only a miracle can save us then we clutch at this straw – and believe in it. If 'they' cannot offer a remedy then understandably many parents, though not ostensibly looking for miracles, are willing to try the latest alternative therapy or cure that comes along. Why not? They have nothing to lose, they might argue. And who knows? At least they will have tried, they will have done their best.

These treatments can range from swimming with dolphins, to large doses of vitamin B6; from following a gluten-free diet to something called Holding Therapy. Of course not all of their proponents claim miraculous results, but the prospect of any improvement is temptation enough and some parents feel they should be prepared to go to the ends of the earth to help their children – literally. The Higashi schools in America and Japan (where they originated) use an approach they call Daily Life Therapy where the pupils are subjected – by English standards though not by Japanese ones – to almost military style behaviour control and extensive physical exercise, the idea being that strict routine gives security to these very fearful children and that lots of vigorous activity burns up destructive energy. No doubt this is effective for some children with autism or for some aspects of the condition and there have been accounts of wonderful results. Yet for any family to send their child to one of these schools, even if the huge sums of money needed were no object, tremendous sacrifices have to be made.

The problem is that a technique that may help one child frequently seems to be ineffective with another. When Gabriel was about 10 years old a huge controversy (in the world of autism) was raging over Holding Therapy. This consisted of forcibly holding one's child for up to 45 minutes despite his or her resistance and distress. Indeed the distress was considered a necessary part of the holding. From being distressed the child could then (theoretically at least) experience being comforted by the mother (usually) and thus begin to 'bond' and build an emotional rapport that had been absent hitherto. Anecdotal accounts abounded citing both amazing successes and dismal failures.

Many well meaning people urged us to try 'holding' with Gabriel. One or two even becoming aggressive when we demurred. All too often we were being told of a programme on the television or an article in a newspaper about a new treatment for autism and it is difficult to keep a balanced and realistic view of what you should or shouldn't pursue. Besides one has to have faith in a method and I had no faith that I could 'hold' Gabriel. Even at that age he was very strong, especially if determined to resist, and I could only foresee an exhausting and traumatic outcome, and not only for myself. Therese Jolliffe writing of her own experience of being held said: 'To me the suffering was terrible and it achieved nothing. Some people who dislike this treatment argue that the children submit out of exhaustion.' According to Temple any beneficial effects were 'mainly due to desensitization of the autistic child's system to touch'. Holding would seem to play the same part as her squeeze machine, except of course that she used her machine voluntarily. Nowadays it might even be considered an abuse of a child's rights to force him or her to submit to such treatment.

Parents must make up their own minds about the lengths they are prepared to go. The Kaufman family of Massachusetts USA devoted some 'three and a half years and 9000 hours' to working with their son – that was all his waking hours, seven days a week. This 'work' entailed as far as possible entering their son's world – twiddling when he twiddled, shouting when he shouted and shredding paper when he shredded. They spent their time with him in a room bare of all distractions eyeball to eyeball (the father having given up his job, and later using volunteers) until the boy began to 'wake up' and eventually 'completely emerged from his autism'.

The Kaufmans called their method the Son-Rise Program (also called here sometimes the Option method or Options) and after their success with their son they went on to work with other parents. The idea behind the method is that by making interaction a pleasurable activity, by making people more attractive than obsessive activities, the child will be encouraged to join 'our world'. Of prime importance is an accepting and loving attitude on the part of the parents, coupled with a great deal of dedication and presumably a willingness to work hard.

The Lovaas method is named after Professor Ivar Lovaas who heads an autism clinic at the University of California LA. As with the previous treatment, enormous effort is required on the part of the parents, who engage in one-to-one intensive behavioural therapy for up to 40 hours a week. Clearly the simple practicalities of pursuing some of these therapies (one family was reported to have spent more than £60,000 on treating their son, while in another the father took a year off work to help with his child) are enough to prevent or deter most parents from any involvement beyond reading about them.

Meanwhile mega-vitamin therapy – high doses of B_6 taken with magnesium – has been claimed to lead to behavioural improvements for some (though a more recent view is that too much B_6 has deleterious effects), while the introduction of a milk and gluten-free diet has allegedly helped others, as has pinpointing and avoiding a variety of allergens. (Donna Williams is convinced that dietary factors were major contributors to her autism.)

Auditory Integration Training was developed by Dr Guy Berard. He invented an electronic device which, by removing some sound frequencies and emphasizing others reconditions the hearing of autistic children so that they are no longer so acutely sensitive to ordinary sounds, thus alleviating the distress of children who are especially vulnerable to sound. Although not claiming to be a cure for autism the treatment has had far-reaching effects for some sufferers.

Facilitated Communication also does not claim to cure but to be a way of getting people to communicate. For those people who suffer from autism and do not speak it was thought that typing could be a way for them of freeing expression. The problem is that a facilitator – another person – aids the autistic person by holding or supporting his or her arm while he/she uses the keyboard. This naturally prompts the question of how much of the resulting communication or material comes from the person pressing the keys and how much originates (even unconsciously) from the facilitator. When one learns that allegations of sexual abuse against families or carers have been made on the basis of information obtained in this way from those who are otherwise unable to communicate, it is easy to see how important it is not to leap to any conclusions. At the same time one must not throw out the baby with the bath water and using a keyboard (without a facilitator) can be a very effective way to help some people with autism. As one young man discovered: 'This once virtually non-communicating person now loves talking through his fingers.'

It is extremely difficult to reach a conclusion about many of these alternative treatments and therapies. New ones appear regularly while others disappear without a trace. (The latest 'dramatic break-through', *The Observer*, September 1998, has been the use of the hormone secretin; again near-miraculous results have been reported.) We struggle to understand our children's puzzling ways, often with the conviction that there must be a key to them, a simple solution if only we could find it and hey presto here we seem to have one. However it is important not to get carried away. The media are constantly presenting us with tales of triumph over tragedy, success against all odds, but the failures never make the news. Yet are we prepared for failure? What about the brothers and sisters who will have to take a back seat, and are both partners (assuming you are two) equally committed? A solid relationship is as important as the necessary funds and dedication before embarking on what could be a wild goose chase.

On the other hand, after having got as much information as possible about a therapy we feel could be helpful and having weighed up all other relevant factors, if we then decide to proceed we must endeavour to balance hope with caution, perseverance with honesty. Who are we doing this for? Gunilla Gerland is in her thirties and suffers from autism. She has written a book entitled *A Real Person* and has this to say:

> The fact that so called normal people, or whatever I should call them, have thought that they know exactly how all human beings function has been one of the harmful things in my life: that those people have a model, into which they have tried to fit me. And that they also have been absolutely convinced that this model of theirs is the only existing model.

If pursuing a particular treatment only brings us nearer to accepting our children as and for what they are, then it will not have been in vain.

13

'Of my life story I know only the middle, not the beginning nor the end' (Urdu couplet)

Something terrible has happened – the worst thing imaginable – Neil has died.

Neil was dead. Inside I screamed, I howled, raged and wept – but was too numb to utter a cry. It was a death on the road, a not uncommon death in the age of the motor car. This was one of those tragedies that everyone knows happens, all too frequently. An unnatural death and one that strikes with random and ruthless suddenness; a death where there has been no time for preparation and no farewell, leaving those behind devastated with shock and grief. So it was with us, as we struggled to take in the dreadful truth. My beloved had left on his bike that beautiful but fateful Sunday morning – 12 June, the day after his 47th birthday – and half an hour later had been knocked off it by a car. He never regained consciousness and died the following day.

My life – our lives – were turned upside down in an instant, I hardly knew which way to turn with the gravity of the situation and through all those terrible hours and early days one panic-stricken thought above all others kept jumping into my head: Gabriel! What am I going to do about Gabriel? How am I going to manage?

To begin with, as soon as I knew Neil had been involved in an accident I had telephoned The Haven for emergency respite care. We didn't know how seriously he had been hurt but assumed we might be at the hospital for days. It was imperative to get Gabriel looked after and he was able to go to The Haven the day after the accident.

During the days following Neil's death when there was so much to be attended to it just wouldn't have been possible with Gabriel around. Now and then as Christian and I set about the practicalities that had to be dealt with we wondered if we should include him in some way, but dismissed the idea as soon as it occurred to us. No, it was out of the question; he was too unruly and, we agreed, he probably wouldn't understand what was happening anyway. It would be better if he stayed at The Haven until after the funeral.

Looking back I'm not sure that I made the right decision. A year later I was to attend the funeral of the daughter of an acquaintance, a young woman with learning difficulties who had died suddenly in her sleep. There were several other learning disabled people in the congregation and although there were a few odd noises and gestures, even the occasional shout during the service, we were all used to that and nobody minded. On the whole they behaved very well and no doubt in their own ways they appreciated being present at an important and moving ceremony. I think now I should have let Gabriel come to the funeral but at the time I felt I had no choice.

On the other hand he still needed to be told and it was his social worker who asked me what I proposed to do about this, asked me how I would explain Neil's death to him and suggested arranging for him to see the body. I agreed and rang The Haven to ask if they would bring Gabriel to our town where Neil's body now lay at the undertaker's. Christian and I met them outside the chapel of rest. Gabriel surely had an idea that there was something gravely wrong – he had been with us as the dreadful events unfolded, through tears and endless telephone calls – and was unusually quiet as he got out of the minibus.

We took him into the little chapel where Neil was lying and I explained that Dad was dead. I took Gabriel's hand and laid it on Neil's so that he could feel it was cold and he just stood there motionless and hushed. No reaching for the leaves and flowers in profusion all around him, no movement, no sound until after a few minutes he walked out. Yet he didn't want to leave, but remained standing outside the door and when I asked 'Do you want to have another look at Dad?' he touched his lips without hesitation. We

Resting during a walk with Neil

Neil keeping an eye on Gabriel in the garden. Twirler flying and still running

returned to Neil and talked about how he took Gabriel for long walks, just the two of them together, and how his dad played with him and chased him and let him sit in the workshop to play with the sawdust, about what a good dad he'd been and how we were all going to miss him terribly, before leaving once again and taking him back to the minibus. Later a member of staff rang to report that he had been very quiet for the rest of the day but that otherwise there had been no problems.

Naturally this was a time of great sadness and turmoil for us all – but at least Christian, Jacob and I could talk to each other about what had happened and could draw comfort from the sympathy of family and friends, whereas it was impossible to know what Gabriel made of it. When he returned home after Neil's funeral his behaviour seemed much as usual, though I was fairly sure that he had some under-standing of what had taken place. We all felt especially helpless faced with his lack of language and ability to communicate.

Meanwhile life had to go on and Christian, knowing the difficulty I would have looking after Gabriel on my own, had already decided to interrupt his university course for a year and return home. One of the main problems was Gabriel's unpredictable and challenging behav-iour outside the home. Even Neil who could control him better than anyone else had more than once to rely on his superior physical strength when he'd blown a fuse in the marketplace. As for me, I had avoided taking him out on my own for several months – ever since the cakeshop incident – and without Christian to help it meant I would be largely confined to the house when Gabriel was home. Not only would I be unable to do errands such as shopping, going to the bank, the doctor's and so on, but I would also be unable to attend meetings, parents' evenings at school (his and Jacob's) and other such necessary appointments. I would confine my social life to times when G was at respite, but on other occasions Christian could 'babysit'.

Added to that, simply the fact that Christian was around meant the psychological burden was shared a little, if not the physical drudgery. I would not ask him to help except when I had to. I didn't expect him to take over Neil's role, but knowing he was there to back me up and could occasionally take over for a couple of hours – even half an hour – was an enormous relief. I was extremely thankful for his decision and don't think I would have been able to manage without him. Fortunately too, he was able to transfer to another university within commuting distance and so continue his studies;

something he hadn't considered when he first proposed to return and which eventually turned out to his benefit.

So now, as far as Gabriel was concerned I was the captain of the ship and I would have to make that clear. We were often asked, even more so after Neil's death, how we controlled our son and I wish to be honest here – at the risk of alienating some of my readers.

Neil and I had always agreed on the subject of corporal punishment. In our view it was simple: smacks were what little children understood best. Some behaviour such as temper tantrums, deliberately naughty behaviour or disobedience were best dealt with by a short sharp smack; not in anger or as a reaction (though that is easily done and I own up to being guilty of it myself), but as an appropriate response and message. That being said however we were not ogres; in fact it was very rarely indeed that either of us ever found reason to administer a salutary smack – at least to our eldest and youngest sons.

But with Gabriel things were different. Saying 'No' as he crawled towards the fire had little effect (we hadn't realised then how limited his understanding of language was); on the other hand a smack didn't work either. He seemed, literally, to have a very thick skin and showed little more reaction to a smack than if a fly had landed on him. Like many children with autism he not only seemed unable to make the connection but also appeared remarkably indifferent to pain. As Lorna Wing writes: 'There are many stories of children with broken bones, dental abscesses, appendicitis or other sources of severe pain who make no complaint and behave as if nothing were amiss.' Donna Williams recounts an incident where she is bitten by a child she is teaching. The bite is a 'funny sensation' and the other teachers, surprised at her lack of reaction, ask "Didn't it hurt you?" "I think so," I responded, not quite sure but sure from their responses that it should have. "You should have said 'ouch', I reminded myself silently. People say 'ouch' if they get bitten."

Yet with a child like Gabriel, his problem with making connections and his lack of understanding (for years he apparently didn't understand 'no') also made other options ineffectual. Being sent to his room was not a punishment (he often disappeared up there for long periods, liking to be alone, or was sent up there to calm down after a 'wobbly'), nor was being deprived of TV, sweets, treats or any of the other common devices most parents use.

So when he was especially 'naughty' a smack would have to do – either with the hand or the wooden spoon – until he learned to make the connection. It was another case of 'constant dripping', of endless repetition until certain boundaries had been established. What behaviour deserved this treatment one might ask? Well, defecating in his room and smearing the results on the carpet and walls did. So did grabbing handfuls of food from someone else's plate during a meal or deliberately decimating the plants or pouring the bottle of cooking oil over his duvet or transferring all the bath water onto the floor.

The trouble was that, as Lorna Wing so rightly points out in her book *The Autistic Spectrum*: 'Many children and adults with autistic disorders find [the outward signs of anger] interesting and rewarding and try to induce them again.' Yet although one had to be careful not to fall into the trap of reacting in a way that perversely he enjoyed (and I cannot over-emphasize the difficulty with someone so maddeningly provocative), Gabriel did learn to make connections. He did come to understand that certain behaviour was unacceptable and would result in punishment even if he had little idea why, and slowly, ever so slowly as he also learned to interpret tones of voice, the smacks got further and further apart.

Nonetheless there were still frequent times when behaviour had to be curbed or prevented. Now that I was alone and Gabriel was getting bigger and stronger and I was getting older and weaker, I could not continue to control him physically. Sometimes I could use guile or reverse psychology ('No Gabriel, you *can't* go to bed yet'), but I knew that in order to get him to respond to me I needed to gain his respect. He, on the other hand, appeared to be testing me and seeing just how far he could push me by being especially confrontational in the weeks that followed Neil's death. I had to stand my ground, to assert myself calmly, firmly, and not waver. Although he is not aggressive, if thwarted he is liable to become like the proverbial mad bull in a china shop and quite alarming, so I had to conquer my fear of any repercussions I might trigger. Occasionally I reinforced my position by fetching the wooden spoon and using it or threatening to use it. Though my brandishing the spoon didn't frighten him, he knew it meant I was getting serious, I was not going to back down and he might as well capitulate. Eventually I found that the more I asserted myself over the following months, the more rarely I had to resort to the spoon. As I grew more confident Gabriel became more co-operative, and in a sense we both came to respect each other's limits. Now (aged 21), he still has a habit of flatly refusing to do as he is asked – get changed, go to bed, etc. – and he often makes his meaning plain by sitting down and refusing to budge. However, if push comes to shove – it's midnight and I'm not prepared to mess about any longer – and I finally fetch the spoon, he takes it firmly out of my hand, returns it to the kitchen drawer and does what is required. But not before initiating a few delaying tactics – running *past* the bathroom, maybe a dozen times, rather than into it – as I stand wearily by calling on all my reserves, or even fetching the spoon again, at which a little smile appears on his face as if to say aha! I'm getting the last word after all, while I am reminded of Lewis Carroll's verse:

> Speak roughly to your little boy
> And beat him when he sneezes.
> He only does it to annoy
> Because he knows it teases.

So there it is. I offer no apologies nor do I offer it as a solution for others. We – and later I – simply did what we felt we had to do in our particular situation, both for his sake and our own.

But however well I was coping with Gabriel for the time being, I couldn't carry on indefinitely or alone. His future needed to be reconsidered and the best solution seemed to be residential care.

The question of residential care had often been raised (somewhat hesitantly) by people who knew us and our problems well. Once, when Gabriel was about 7 and had been more challenging than usual, I overheard Neil's mother say to his father, 'They'll have to put him away.' 'Over my dead body,' retorted Neil when I told him later. For it was true we never seriously considered it; not because of some heroic decision, more a question of circumstance.

I have often wondered how it must be when one has to face the fact that there is something wrong with one's baby at birth; coming to terms with it during the vulnerable aftermath of pregnancy and birth, amid shattered dreams and expectations – how do you do it? In the past you were often urged to 'forget about the baby, dear' and to leave it behind. Today attitudes have changed and, though not unheard of, that is rarely an option. And rightly. Nonetheless acceptance takes time and is painful and most parents have little help through this difficult period.

With autism however it's not like that. There is no intimation at birth that the baby is anything but normal. It is true a few mothers (and presumably fathers too) do feel very early on there is 'something not quite right' about their child, something that worries them. Sometimes he – it is most often 'he' – is too quiet, too 'good'; sometimes he is the opposite, screaming interminably and incon- solably. Sometimes he appears to develop normally, is potty-trained and starting to talk when he inexplicably changes and starts to regress behaviourally and forgets any speech he may have acquired. But all of these are the exceptions. In a survey carried out by the NAS nearly three-quarters of parents of children with autism had no suspicions of anything amiss during their child's first year, and less than a third of the children had been diagnosed autistic by the end of their third year.

So it was more or less with Gabriel. By the time we knew he may have suffered from autism we had been living with it and him for three years. By then he was firmly entrenched as one of the family, ours, and whether by fate or accident, our responsibility. We did as the vast majority of parents do in such situations, we simply got on with it. This is not to say that 'getting on with it' doesn't require heroic efforts at times but that the strength of the parent–child relationship (even when the child is not your own blood, but adopted – which happens) makes getting on with it the only option; one of the good sides of human nature.

Fortunately nature also instils hope; hope that 'they' will find a cure or that the miracle will happen and our child will recover spontaneously. As long as we have hope we can be optimistic about the future and meanwhile cope with the challenge of the present. This challenge too, to swim rather than sink, to put on brave faces and try to be philosophical, brings its own strengths and rewards. 'I'm sure I couldn't do it,' people often say, before pausing and adding, 'but I suppose I would if I had to.' And so they inevitably would.

It goes without saying that a good relationship lightens the burden immeasurably and as I have made clear Neil did more than his fair share of taking care of Son Number Two. Fundamentally a deeply spiritual person whose main direction in life was self-understanding and knowledge, as Neil saw it Gabriel provided us with an opportunity to grow, to examine ourselves and our lives, and rather than rail against him we should thank him for it. This unusual way of looking at things was one I admit I frequently found difficult to share, however much I might recognise the wisdom of it. It was difficult not to wrinkle my nose and screw up my face in disgust as I dealt with Gabriel's dirty bottom, but I saw the sense in not 'wasting energy in negative emotions' as Neil put it. I learned to stifle my impatience when I had to jump up and down a dozen times to attend to him when I was practically asleep on my feet and longing to sit down and relax. 'He's helping us not to be lazy,' Neil would say, 'and anyway who wants an easy life?' I perished such an unworthy thought. 'Besides,' he concluded, 'Gabriel has a far from easy time himself and what could we do more useful in life than helping him and ourselves?' Changing the facts of the situation was not possible; changing one's attitude was. It was a question of what Neil called 'enlightened self-interest'.

All of this didn't stop both of us feeling a multitude of negative emotions – anger, frustration, resentment, self-pity – but they had to be recognised and addressed. Sometimes one had to admit defeat and I vividly remember once, after Gabriel had been home a few days with some minor illness, taking him into school, bursting into tears and desperately begging them to let him stay for the rest of the day. His teacher disappeared, returning a few minutes later to tell me she had arranged for Gabriel to go into respite care (for the very first time) that weekend. From that time on I was ready to ask for help, to accept respite care without feeling guilty or that at not yet 5 years old he was too young. A relationship with these extremely difficult children is often one of love and hate. 'I still resent him,' one dedicated father confessed to me with disarming honesty, speaking of his very demanding (adopted) autistic son. Kenneth is now in his thirties and in residential care but comes home frequently for the weekend 'so we don't forget what it's like,' his wife told me.

So we lived our lives and despite everything there were still plenty of opportunities to live a creative and satisfying life, both with and without Gabriel. It was far from being all doom and gloom (whatever impression I might have given to the contrary) and we and our other two boys had our share of fun and were happy. Yet as the full extent of Gabriel's disabilities were revealed, as it became obvious that he could never be independent, never live in sheltered housing or pursue any kind of meaningful occupation, the question of residential care at some time was a foregone conclusion – if only for the fact he would probably outlive us. Where he would go and when we were not sure, but felt that an appropriate time would be when he reached his early twenties and Jacob would also be leaving home. Now that time would have to be brought forward.

A few days after Neil's death I came across Benny, the local simpleton. Often to be seen lying beside the canal towpath sucking a straw and watching the boats go by, or once spotted by a friend of mine wandering naked around the town allotments, Benny seemed to know instinctively that Gabriel was a fellow spirit. We always said hello when we passed him on our ramblings. Dirty and dishevelled, I now saw him basking in the sun on a bench in the churchyard.

'Hello Benny. You know Gabriel, don't you? And his dad? He died, Benny.'

'Ohhh,' sadly. Long silence. Then worriedly, 'You ain't goin' to put 'im away, are yer?'

'Well Benny, I'll have to. He's not like you. I just can't look after him alone.'

And so finally, over Neil's dead body, I started to think about Gabriel leaving home.

14

Dark days

After Neil's funeral Gabriel returned to a subdued and shaken family, yet he himself showed no obvious signs of grief or sorrow. Whether this was because he was unable to comprehend what had happened, or whether this was due to his autism and lack of feeling for others was impossible to say. A boy with Asperger's syndrome on being asked how he was getting on since the death of his mother was reported to have said that there was no need to worry since because of his condition he was less vulnerable to such losses. It certainly didn't stop Gabriel being as mischievous as ever, jumping out of a bedroom window onto the porch, the car and into the street the very day he came home (it was hot and we'd got careless). A day or two later as I relaxed in the garden while he was indoors I happened to glance up and to my horror saw him on the point of climbing out of the loft window onto the roof. Christian raced upstairs and just managed to catch hold of his feet and pull him back in. I screwed the window shut with a very large screw.

Monday 4 July

To school to talk about G's future. I am worried about him going to the local college in September (which still isn't 100% sure anyway) and then having to move again soon after to a residential place. To my surprise and before I had voiced my anxiety, the Head offered to keep Gabriel on at school for another year while we looked for somewhere residential, so that he would only have to make one move, and that not straight away. She was sure the rules could be stretched and in any case by next July he would only be three months over the leaving deadline. It seems his teacher (who over the years has become one of his fans) first made the suggestion knowing how unsettling it might be for him. I was touched by their thoughtfulness and support for both Gabriel and myself.

We made arrangements to meet with social worker and careers officer as soon as possible to discuss the options (yet another meeting) and I left for home feeling several pounds lighter.

The question now is where to begin. The advantage – if I may use that word here – of having a child as handicapped and challenging as Gabriel is that everyone who has anything to do with him from social services and education is agreed that funding has to be provided for him. The disadvantage is that the more 'difficult' the client, the fewer the available places. To quote from that spring issue of *Communication*: 'At present there are no specialised services in the UK for people with autism who exhibit severe behaviour disorders.' (The NAS was about to open a new home for just such individuals – but it would be too late for Gabriel even if he should qualify.)

Ideally, like all parents, I would like to find somewhere near – by which I mean within an hour's drive. It must be secure, with good-hearted and energetic staff, preferably fairly spacious and ideally in a rural environment. Although modern thinking tends to the view that clients are best placed in smaller family-sized units I was not sure that was important. Houses 'in the community' might be fine for more able people with learning difficulties, but I could not really envisage Gabriel participating in local life – darts down at the pub, discos, shopping at the supermarket. Beyond the necessities of food and shelter his requirements are modest. Music is important, so is a plentiful supply of twirlers. He enjoys walks and drives and seems happier where there is space both indoors and out, either to work off his energy or be alone – but that's about it. Simple requirements, but would they be easy to satisfy?

Of course I wanted somewhere near. The nearer he was, the easier it would be to visit him or to have him home regularly. Carers come and carers go, other residents, staff and volunteers come and go. Over the years many, many people look after our children and pass through their lives never to be seen again. Only the family remains a constant with the well-being of our children forever our concern. The nearer Gabriel was, the easier it would be to see he was all right, happy. Perhaps it has always been so, but lately more than ever it seemed there were reports of people in care being abused by their carers. There had even been a recent case at school and a member of staff had been suspended for mistreating the children in her care. It had shocked and disturbed not only the parents of the children concerned but the other parents too. Although Gabriel was not one of the pupils involved (and we felt that even if he had been he was not easily intimidated and would probably have emerged unscathed) we were angry too.

People with learning difficulties are especially vulnerable and with limited language or none at all such abuse could pass unnoticed for years, as indeed it had here. (The added and common factor of other staff being afraid to blow the whistle also delayed discovery.) As parents we are only too aware of the enormous demands our children make on the patience and goodwill of the staff we entrust them to. Yet trust them we must and when that trust is broken we feel we have let our sons and daughters down. While being near is no guarantee that such abuse can't happen, it might lessen the odds.

As I bathed Gabriel tonight I noticed all the scuffs and scratches with which his body is habitually marked. His eye was bruised where he had slipped and banged it on the edge of the bath. The back of his neck and forehead were covered with minute scabs where he had pinched himself in distress. There were bruises and scratches on his body, presumably acquired in such escapades as scrambling over fences or through windows. His knuckles were calloused and cracked from obsessive autistic tapping and there was a cut on one finger. There were burn scars on his legs and feet from previous accidents and his thighs were bruised where he had slapped himself in a recent big mood. He always has a multitude of cuts and grazes on his body and often we have no idea how he got them. He doesn't ask for them to be attended to (except rarely, perhaps a splinter under the nail) and they often pass unnoticed until bath-time.

Tonight I am confident all of these injuries have been acquired either in the rough and tumble of Gabriel's daily life or have been self-inflicted but, and this is the point, I could so easily be wrong.

Tuesday 5 July

Gabriel ate an entire pound of cherries after school, stones and all. Typical. Later he wandered round the garden for a long time with a clothes peg clipped on his tongue. We all tried it and couldn't tolerate it for more than a few seconds and wondered why he should do such a thing. This was unlike the self-injury arising from distress or anger which we often see. He even appeared to enjoy the sensation. Donna says that she hurt herself in order to test *whether she was actually real*, to make herself feel something and confirm her existence. She also wrote: 'Everything I did, from holding two fingers together to scrunching up my toes, had a meaning, usually to do with reassuring myself that I was in control and no one could reach me.' Was that what the tea-strainer balanced on the back of the neck signified?

Thursday 7 July

Have been having trouble asserting myself especially since I'm still feeling very fragile. Paper tearing has been a long-standing occupation of Gabriel's. Pointless to forbid it, tissues and toilet paper I allow, but books are another matter. To give him his due, as with the plants he has mostly learned to limit himself – to just one leaf, one petal, one corner of a page, which he tears into smaller and smaller pieces – and many books have a page somewhere with a missing corner, as if to say 'Gabriel woz here'.

Tonight I was looking through a photograph album when he suddenly and deliberately tore a corner off and ruined a picture of Neil. But instead of feeling angry and remonstrating with him, he had touched a soft spot and I could only cry. Yet my tears mean nothing to him, nothing at all. He has no idea how I feel and doesn't care, and probably as far as he is concerned I am just making a funny noise. He is not interested in me, or anyone else, except as providers of his needs. His world is totally self-obsessed. Later still we had another incident.

Keys play a large part in our lives and one aspect of respite we appreciate the most is not having to bother with them: keys to the bedrooms, keys to the kitchen cupboards, to the bathroom, the front door, the back door, the windows, the wardrobe, and so on. Gabriel has not really mastered turning a key nor does he recognise the different keys, but occasionally he gets lucky if he finds one I've hidden, which was the case tonight. In the space of two minutes while I was on the lavatory (Mr Exasperating never misses a chance) he got the washing-up liquid out of a locked cupboard, emptied all of it on the table, then, silly boy, after smearing it liberally over the furniture and himself, rubbed it in his eyes. As I skidded across the floor I was tempted to get the wooden spoon but decided discretion was the better part of valour and instead coaxed him into the bath, which he got into with all his clothes on, while I cleared up. There were bubbles here, bubbles there, bubbles absolutely everywhere. The bathroom was a blizzard of bubbles as I cleared up and tried to bathe his eyes with clean water. They were evidently very sore and he kept rubbing them with anything he could find – dirty dishcloths, old socks – ignoring offers of help or clean cloths.

Friday 8 July

Eyes in such a state had to keep him home. Puffy and swollen and obviously painful he couldn't open one at all. He looked dreadful. Yet, and this is hard to credit, he later found some washing up liquid again, poured it in his hands and rubbed it on them. Sometimes I can't make sense of him at all.

Monday 18 July

To visit a place for Gabriel with social worker and careers officer. It is only 30 miles away, a large establishment for about 80 residents who live in small units scattered about the very spacious grounds. There are greenhouses, workshops and a farm where they work. As I looked round I was impressed: Crafts, Snoezelen, Drama, Cookery,

Computers, and lots more. In one of the workshops several residents, mostly male, were seated round a large table doing needlework. When I expressed my doubts about Gabriel engaging in this activity the teacher, a mild-mannered, middle-aged woman told me she hadn't 'come across a client yet who couldn't learn to use a needle'. Really?! There were large bags of wool in the next room reminding me of a time I'd had to make a hasty exit with Gabriel from a wool shop before anyone noticed the mass of skeins he'd managed to tangle inextricably in the space of an eye blink.

Looking at the residents however Gabriel seems no better or worse than most of them and I know that one of the units is specifically for those with autism (the one surrounded by a high fence) so feeling cautiously optimistic we decide to go for it. In fact there are no places available at the moment but since all the wheels grind exceedingly slowly in these matters – funding must be applied for, meetings held, assessments carried out – a place should come up in the meantime. The social worker would feel happier if I didn't count on anything and advises me to look at some other places as well, which I promise to do. She is retiring next year and getting Gabriel settled somewhere is one assignment she is determined to complete.

Thursday 21 July

Just as Gabriel was about to leave for school this morning he fell to the floor and started fitting so had to send the taxi off without him.

It is now several weeks since he started to have the anti-convulsants normally prescribed for epilepsy and so far they have had little effect. A second and now a third drug have been added to the original prescription and the doses have been monitored and tweaked – more of one, less of another and so on – but they have not diminished the frequency of the seizures. There is also the not inconsiderable problem of getting him to take the medication. The tablets have to be crushed and hidden in food, but this is an area where all Gabriel's intelligence comes to the fore. He's certainly sharp enough to notice me doctoring his meals and it has to be done very surreptitiously so that he doesn't suspect anything. But then he might only eat half of the meal or none of it, his eating habits being as unreliable as his other ones. Also, since his sense of taste is probably more acute than average, no doubt he often rejects food because of the medication (he is not to know it is for his own good, only that it tastes horrible). At the end of each day it's difficult to know exactly how much of the dose has been taken.

The only noticeable effect of the anti-convulsants has been to make him rather drowsy, which interferes with his bowel movements, which leads to laxatives being prescribed, which are equally – no, more – problematical to administer, which means a build-up of toxins leading to further fits (according to some), which means a higher dose of anti-convulsants, which makes him sleepier still. As one care worker sympathised, it's all a 'vicious circus'. But it's early days yet and of course I'd be delighted if the seizures could be controlled.

The end of term is approaching and I wonder how we'll manage through the summer hols without my helpmate Neil. As usual there is a play scheme for the first three weeks running at a school only a few minutes' walk from our house; that and a few short stays at The Haven should see us through. Just take it a day at a time and go with the flow.

I deposit Gabriel every morning with a packed lunch and a change of clothes or two. The play scheme is mostly staffed by volunteers – lots of enthusiastic young people usually who enjoy the camaraderie and the many activities and outings that are arranged. Picnics, barbecues, bouncy castles and real castles, the organisers and helpers exhaust themselves daily in their efforts to give the children a good time. They go to the zoo yet again, much to Jacob's envy, this being about Gabriel's tenth visit there and, as his brother points out, 'He probably doesn't even look at the animals'.

He is well known to the organisers and is allocated a pleasant and mature young man as his 'minder'. Ian is filling in time between school and university where he is about to start a degree in medicine. His only sibling, a younger sister, is multiply handicapped and he is no stranger to the task of caring. I am sure Gabriel couldn't be in better hands. In fact he must have enjoyed the play scheme more than ever this year – thanks certainly in part to Ian – as a few days after it had finished he disappeared over the gate one day. After a frantic half-hour spent scouring the high street (checking out sweetshop and bakery) and the towpath we finally tracked him down in the school playground, which he was most reluctant to leave. Returning home I repressed all thought of the very busy road he had crossed to get there and switched myself on to red alert for the rest of the day.

But it's a constant challenge to keep one jump ahead of The Phenomenon. Although the loft window was now firmly secured and all his attempts to open it had failed, Gabriel hadn't put it out of his mind. One day he again vanished from the garden where he had been only moments before. I ran up the road in search of him when my heart suddenly stopped as, looking back, I saw him silhouetted against the sky on the roof of the house looking down the chimney. Not only is he like a cat with nine lives, but he is as agile as a cat too. He must have *run* up the back of the house using the drainpipe to clamber onto the roof where, well pleased with himself at outwitting us and being out of our reach, he was nonchalantly exploring this new territory.

What to do? I couldn't get up there, while Christian was wary about going after him and the episode developing into a chase. Gabriel might decide to jump the three-foot gap onto the next house and slip (I broke out in a sweat at the thought), or the rickety drainpipe or gutter might give way and they could both fall. Did he have no sense of danger or was he so sure-footed that we were worrying needlessly? Should we call the fire brigade? Or would more attention only prompt calamity? Calmly he peered down the chimney – he wouldn't think of getting into it would he? This thought prompted another outbreak of sweat – as he then walked back and forth along the ridge fiddling with a thread from his jumper. A neighbour telephoned to ask whether I knew Gabriel was up there and to tell me how dangerous it was – as if I didn't know. Still no point in panicking and I unscrewed and opened the loft window in the hope that if we ignored him he would find his way back in. At last, after what seemed an interminable time but was in fact about half an hour, when he had fully satisfied his curiosity and it appeared that no one was interested in his latest exploit, that is what he did. He climbed back in safe and sound, while I, once the pressure was off, turned to jelly.

Yet on other days he stumbles about the house like a zombie, dozes on and off and hardly moves. At least on these days one can relax (though a quiet day often presages a noisy night). However, for some reason known only to himself he has taken to sleeping in his room again at night, after about two years on the kitchen-diner floor – a welcome spin-off as it will be more convenient when we get our dog.

'Oh, and get him a dog,' was the parting advice from one medical man we consulted about Gabriel when he was about 2 years old, his reasoning being that if our son wouldn't relate to people he would relate to an animal. But although at the time we gave careful consideration to this piece of pop psychology, the circumstances of our lives were such – cramped rented accommodation, desperate financial straits and a very uncertain future – that we decided we couldn't take on the extra responsibility of a pet. However, only days after Neil's death Jacob wistfully asked if we could now have a dog. Knowing how he had always hankered after one, this seemed a good time to agree to it and today (while Gabriel is at respite) we are collecting Max from a rescue centre. A cross between a collie and a hearth rug Max 'ain't got a bad thought in 'is 'ead' according to the proprietor of the dog's home; it will be interesting to see what Gabriel's reaction is when he returns.

Well, very little reaction at all. Apart from half-heartedly fiddling with the dog's tail and poking a finger in his eyes (Max truly hasn't got a bad thought in his head – except towards cats) Gabriel has mostly ignored him. The dog on the other hand quickly realised the wisdom of keeping a low profile when he is around. He is also nervous when Gabriel gets into one of his moods and is obviously sensitive to the tension he generates. Otherwise he has fitted in well and although according to Jacob, 'life is much better with a dog', it doesn't look as if having a dog is going to have a significant effect on

The Lad – and I feel sure it probably would have made no difference if we'd had one all those years ago.

A pity. It would be wonderful if there were something that would alleviate Gabriel's present distress. Now back at school he is once again going through 'a bad patch'. Although his whole life has been a roller-coaster of good patches and bad patches he seems to be more inward and cut off from us than ever just now and all of his mischievous sparkle has faded into non-existence. Is grief the cause? It surely must be partly to blame. Neil gave Gabriel so much attention, played with him, teased him, took him out, that perhaps it is only now, three months after his death that Gabriel is feeling the full impact of the loss. Although he may appear to care very little for others or to value their love for him, perhaps this is evidence that those feelings do exist. Added to that he is at that period of life which most young people find disturbing – adolescence – and his hormones must be affecting him as they affect other teenagers. Drugs, grief, adolescence and the dark, silent forces of autism – no wonder he is dazed, unhappy and confused. No wonder he pinches himself until he bleeds and pinches those around him. (This week he came home in the taxi one afternoon with his hands tied together to prevent this. Shades of Bedlam!) He's been so unapproachable and isolated lately that it hurts and we all long to see him smile.

Tonight he didn't appear to look at any of us all evening. When he had a bath and I washed and dried his face I tried to get him to look at me but he just couldn't bear to. Simply shut his eyes when I got too close.

Yet I know that this too will pass and know from past experience that often two steps backwards precede three steps forward. I sincerely hope so – for one of the backward steps has been a return to nappies during the day. Merde!

15

Shit happens

It would be easy to skim over the subject of shit, crap, poo, excrement or whatever you like to call it. Easy not to mention the un-mentionable in deference to the sensibilities of my readers. But since I wish to paint as accurate a portrait of Gabriel as possible and since it is an aspect of our lives with him that has occupied untold amounts of time and energy, I feel it cannot be ignored. Certainly we parents and all those who care for Gabriel and his like cannot afford to be squeamish or to turn our noses up, so to speak, when confronted with the matter.

It is axiomatic that children with learning disabilities do not function normally and therefore many have difficulties with toileting – though with time the majority do achieve some if not complete independence. And maybe Gabriel will one day. We've always been optimistic and he's 'only' 16, but so far we and all his carers have achieved no more success in taming his bottom than we have in socialising him generally. Probably less. Gabriel has remained firmly at the anal stage.

To begin with, in the early years he produced copious amounts and we and the other carers who shared the endless task of keeping him clean joked about our wholefood diet – the effects of wholemeal cereals, beans, lentils and plenty of fresh fruit and vegetables. Five or six BMs (bowel movements) a day were normal and 'Gabriel smells!' a regular call to action. Of course we tried to train him, tried praise and reward and didn't scold or punish, but he was apparently oblivious to what came out of his rear end (only very rarely investigating or playing with it – thank heavens) and as with so many things was unable to make the connections. Optimistically we felt that with encouragement sooner or later he would 'just do it'. Perhaps we were too laid back, perhaps lazy, perhaps too versed in all the psychobabble surrounding shit that we didn't want to get heavy. Instead we just sighed, pulled on the rubber gloves, made a wisecrack about the Augean stables and lit another incense stick to mask the noxious fumes. At least we could thank the powers that be for free pads (delivered 300 at a time and necessitating extra storage space) and a good washing machine and hope that when he went to school the experts would have more success.

Naturally every teacher of every class put toiletting at the top of their list of objectives for Gabriel, and every credit must be given to those who got him dry. But although he soon used the lavatory unprompted when he needed a wee (always sitting down) he refused to use it when he opened his bowels. Psychologists, psychiatrists, doctors and nurses, social workers, fellow parents, friends and family – all have been consulted and have advised, but to no avail. If we'd had £30,000 or more to spare I suppose we could have sent him to the Higashi School for some Daily Life Therapy for a year. There the incontinent child is taught to wash his own clothes and change him or herself. 'We had one boy who came to us at the age of 14 who was still incontinent. He was very hyperactive. But after three months he was calm and able to look after his own needs. "Be a gentleman," I would say to him,' the Head was quoted as saying. Be a gentleman, Gabriel! According to her it works – though one cannot expect any improvement for 'at least three years'.

In fact for us matters took a turn for the worse when Gabriel was about 10 and one teacher decided, with our co-operation, to make yet another attempt to tackle the – er – issue. We all agreed we would haul him off to the loo whenever it was obvious (and it was) he was about to 'perform'. None of us however had bargained for Gabriel's obduracy. So determined was he not to co-operate – at least that's how it appeared – that he would deliberately 'hold' his faeces for lengths of time beyond belief. Unwittingly we had made the situation worse. Much worse.

Now the communications back and forth between home and school and home and respite were full of references to laxatives, suppositories and enemas and our whole lives seemed to revolve around Gabriel's BMs. Would it never cease? Was it a question of 'can't' or 'won't'? Was he so lacking in intelligence that he simply couldn't understand what was required of him, or was it stubbornness in the face of our attempts at coercion? Or maybe it was some inexplicable fear, perhaps a fear of losing a part of himself that prevented him from co-operating? Was it a desire to hold onto something of his own? Was it – is it, for the situation is ongoing – one of the few ways he can exercise control and self-determination? Ah! if only we knew. If only he could tell us. Like other aspects of his behaviour one can't help thinking that there is a key somewhere waiting to be found, but it is becoming increasingly elusive.

And so we come to the present moment when, as a result of years of desperate constipation (walking on tiptoes with stomach drawn in and buttocks clenched) he has reached a state – there's no way to put this delicately – where he oozes shit more or less continuously. Now Gabriel always smells, is always soiled. So after years of him being dry and nappy-free during the day, I am forced to put him back in pads; it is simply impractical not to.

I feel very cast down by this backward step, as much for his sake as my own.

PS A little calculating reveals that at three dirty nappy changes a day (a very conservative estimate) for the sixteen and a half years he has lived with us adds up to more than EIGHTEEN THOUSAND clean ups. Need I say more?

I have been, at social worker's insistence, to visit another residential place for Gabriel. It's a long way away – at least three hours drive in a good car, about four in my old Lada and probably nearer six using public transport – which prejudices me against it from the start. After all if he is going to be there for life how will I be able to keep close contact with my son without eventually moving nearby? Although Neil and I had always thought that the time when Gabriel left home would be the time to move house and that we would choose our next location according to where he was, now I am single I would prefer to stay where I am (as would his brothers). However, apart from the distance a far more disturbing fact was the security, or rather the lack of it, with a busy dual-carriageway running along one boundary of the very large site and the front gates wide open. Students were wandering about from building to building. What was to stop them wandering out of the front gate and, heaven forbid, underneath a car? Obviously these students were not the wandering types but I knew I could not possibly consider it as an option for Gabriel – so am still hoping that choice number one comes up trumps.

A visit today from social worker and occupational therapist to check out if there is any way we can keep Gabriel off the roof. This has become more and more problematical lately and worries me a lot – especially vis-à-vis my neighbours, but I also fear for G's safety. What if he had a fit up there? Now that he cannot get out of the windows he has developed his climbing skills as well as his skills as an agent provocateur. I guess he's not exceptional. I recently saw a programme on TV where an autistic boy had to be rescued from the top of an electricity pylon and knew of another child who frequently got stuck up trees. Donna Williams described how she liked to swing upside down at the top of the highest trees as a young girl, causing panic among the onlookers. Although many people with autism can be afraid of (to us) the most unthreatening things, they can be equally fearless of dangerous situations. (Yet on reflection is there anything less irrational in a fear of, say, spiders as opposed to hoovers? And what about the many non-autistic people who enjoy risking their lives in such activities as motor racing or rock climbing? It is not quite the same of course – people who are afraid of spiders know the fear is irrational and those who take risks calculate the danger.) In Gabriel's case damage to the neighbour's property is a very real concern and for that reason alone he cannot be allowed to range freely over the roofs. Both professionals are sympathetic as we discuss ways in which this might be prevented and whether social services would foot the bill. The occupational therapist warns me however that it will be a long process (I don't doubt it) and that in the meantime I will just have to do my best to be alert. Fortunately winter is approaching which means less time is spent out in the garden and, you never know, the urge to climb might fade.

End of October and another half-term has come and gone, this time almost painlessly. He's been a really good boy. Happy, calm, co-operative. Coming to the bathroom to be changed without having to be asked 25 times or running off in the middle of the operation, eating in a (relatively) civilised manner, enjoying walks along the towpath and drives in the car. Although he didn't sleep for couple of nights at least he didn't pass them running noisily round his bedroom (the foam having been removed a few months ago and the bed reinstalled – even if he does still prefer the floor most nights). To my immense relief he hardly looked at the roof nor attempted to scale the drainpipe but spent a great amount of time in the workshop which I'm sure he associates with Neil. Busily he trotted back and forth to it, his coat on upside down with the hood hanging over his behind, making small noises of pleasure and fiddling away to his heart's content. When catching hold of him one day, I said 'How about a kiss then, Gabriel?' he amazed me by actually offering his cheek and letting me give him one. A red letter day indeed!

Perhaps at last he's coming out of that long unhappy spell and getting over the turmoil caused by his father's death. Everything is so different when he is like this and before I know it I forget about the bad days and start to think that maybe he could continue to live at home after all. I'm not happy about sending him away from the family home and whoever looks after him will surely not understand his little ways as we do. He's so helpless and such a lovable chap at bottom (though not as regards his actual bottom, I have to add) and, and, and so on. But hold on a minute, I'm getting carried away. He would still have to go somewhere during the day and the local day centre for people with learning difficulties definitely isn't suitable, while the all-essential respite care is far more limited for adults than for those under 18. Sorrowfully I admit to myself it's not really a possibility, but can't help feeling pangs of guilt and anxiety at the thought of his future.

Age 15. In a world of his own. Does he think? This picture was in The Independent 1.9.95

'Of course in the old days,' I often hear it said when I voice my thoughts, 'people like Gabriel were looked after by the community.' The whole village or street knew the local imbecile and watched out for him. (One is reminded of Peter the Wild Boy who wandered at will.) But while this was undoubtedly the case for many Gabriels, Peters and others, there have always been some unfortunate souls who for one reason or another have had to be looked after in institutions. It is probably true that the community is much more fractured than in those imagined golden days, but also the environment has become a much more dangerous place. I shudder at the thought of Gabriel being let loose to cross roads, explore railway lines or climb electricity pylons.

Early November

I telephone the college I have applied to for Gabriel to find out what is happening about our application. Six weeks have passed with no news. The woman I speak to tells me a place has just come up in the autistic group and asks if I would like Gabriel to be considered for it. Of course I answer yes and she tells me his name will be put forward for assessment. I'm (foolishly?) pinning my hopes on it. I know I can't continue indefinitely, especially after a recent series of broken nights.

There is nothing like lack of sleep to wear you down. What a relief I feel sometimes when he goes off to school in the mornings. Last night he came to life at midnight (when I had finally got him in his bedroom), tapping and running, jumping and laughing, he carried on until 3 o'clock. I could have strangled him. I know he can't help it, but neither can I, and there seems no rhyme or reason to it. Why does Gabriel take so long to get to sleep when he should be tired? How many times have other carers or teachers said to me 'He should sleep well tonight, he's had a really active day – walked five miles, been out in the minibus, in the pool for an hour, etc.' and it doesn't make the slightest difference. He can sleep for 24 hours or stay awake for 48 hours, driving me into the ground with exhaustion.

Yet to know all is to forgive all, as the saying goes, and both Donna Williams and Therese Joliffe write of how they feared sleep and the dark. Therese says the fearfulness of her autism never leaves her, even in sleep, and affects her dreams. Donna says that for many years she was so terrified of sleep, of losing control, that she tried to sleep with her eyes open. 'Sleep was not a secure place,' she says. Gabriel doesn't sound fearful when he stays awake, but is it possible his activity is a warding off device, a way of keeping demons at bay? Or is his internal clock simply out of order? I wonder. There are so many unanswerable questions when it comes to autism. It does appear however that a lot of the behaviour of autistic people is governed by fear and that they are, as someone put it, in a state of 'permanent jeopardy'.

What about drugs then to help him sleep? Would there be any harm in giving him the odd sleeping pill? And while we're about it some tranquillisers to slow him down during the day? Don't think we haven't considered it. Despite it being against our basic principles, we have. But sufferers from autism appear to be notoriously resistant to such treatment and after a long and informative consultation with a sympathetic doctor some years ago, on balance, according to him, the side-effects seemed to outweigh the possible benefits and for the time being at least we decided to let things be. Now, with maturity, Gabriel is far less active during the day than he was as a young child. As he is receiving medication for his epilepsy (which also slows him down) it might not be a good idea to add other drugs to his regime unless absolutely necessary.

This is not to say that intervention is always inappropriate. Temple Grandin found that an anti-depressant had its uses. She found it calmed her, made her more relaxed and able to get on better with other people. Yet she also recognised that although she was not so driven 'much of the fervour' of her life has gone. For her the cost has been worth it and, most importantly, she is able to decide for herself whether she wishes to use the drug or not. Too often people suffering from learning disabilities are prescribed such drugs as a way of controlling them and making life easier for their carers.

Mid-November

Social worker rings to find out what is happening about Gabriel's placement. Nothing, by all accounts. Apparently no letter about the possible place has been received. The woman dealing with it is on a week's leave. There are problems because of his age (many places will not accept clients under 18, which is an added difficulty in Gabriel's case). But we went into that at the start. What is the matter with these people? Whoever you need to speak to is either on holiday, on a course or in a meeting. Messages are not passed on, phone calls are never returned, forms lost, etc., etc., and all the time precious days and weeks are slipping by.

Big screams and headbanging tonight and a tussle on the wet muddy lawn because he didn't want to come in, although he had been out for more than an hour and it was dark and raining. He frightened the dog and roused the neighbours. All clothes had to taken off and washed and mud wiped off floors, walls and windows. These incidents remind me that I'm not getting any younger or stronger and that they are exactly why we are looking for a place for him away from home. (I must have been crazy the other week to let any thought of him staying at home even enter my mind.) Never mind, it's off to The Haven tomorrow for three nights – though no doubt if he's in the same mood there I shall hear about it. They'll let me know how difficult it is for them and how they have to limit the intake of other clients when Gabriel is there; they can only cope with one difficult one at a time. So what? If they find it such a problem, how do they think I manage? After all it's because of this sort of behaviour that we need respite, because of him they have their jobs. Anyway the place is supposed to be for clients with challenging behaviour. Not too challenging though. Wimps.

Of course I daren't say any of this when I depend so much on their goodwill, for fear of rubbing them up the wrong way (and I do appreciate their help really, just feeling a bit jaded from lack of sleep). I can only hope he doesn't do anything drastic, hope even that he turns on the charm. As is sometimes the way, he isn't too keen to go there – at least that's how I interpret his reluctance to get out of the car when we arrive. I open the passenger door and he climbs into the boot. I go round to the boot and he climbs into the front and we carry on like this playing cat and mouse for ten minutes or so until at last he jumps out and runs inside. After a quick run-down to staff on his medication, his BMs or lack of them (he has been suffering the mother of all constipations) and his present mood (perhaps a connection there?), as usual once I have deposited him there the weight rolls off my shoulders as I roll out of the drive.

Christian and Jacob both remark that evening on how calm and relaxed it is without G at home. There is a palpable difference in the atmosphere and I realise how disturbing it must be for them too and that though they usually shut themselves in their rooms to study they cannot shut out the vibrations. Yet strangely we all agree we'd probably miss him after a while. He has the ability to bring out both the best and the worst in one – feelings of anger and resentment alternating with those of compassion and concern. One doesn't have to examine one's conscience too deeply to know which feelings should be developed.

Early December

The social worker and I are still trying to chase up the residential college. They deny all knowledge of a certain crucial letter – but careers officer has a copy so we know it was sent. As for the telephone conversation about the place in the autistic unit, I think I must have dreamt it. It appears the place has already been allocated to someone else and that Gabriel was not even considered. Someone somewhere is not doing their job and I'm learning far too late that I should make a note of every communication, every conversation and get the name of every person I have to deal with. Oh yes, it's uphill every inch of the way in this game. However, social worker finally achieves success after a number of irate calls and two appointments have been made: one to visit and assess Gabriel at his present school before the end of term and the other at the beginning of January when he will be observed for a day at the college. At last. But I've learnt my lesson and I'm not now counting on anything.

16

Turkeys don't cry

Gabriel has a new obsession – he spent the weekend trying to lie on the clothes line. By hanging onto the shed (to which it was attached at one end) he was able to haul himself up and stretch along it. It looked most uncomfortable and as if he was in danger of emasculating himself as he wobbled precariously before falling off and trying again. I wouldn't have minded except that there was washing hanging out to dry the other end and of course the inevitable happened – the line broke and the washing was dragged down to the ground. Now with no line to climb onto, he transferred his attention to the sitting-room door. That was much easier to get onto and balance on and he installed himself on top of the door several times, staying up there for half an hour or so. In between worrying about the strain on the hinges and expecting the door to fall off I wondered if there was any explanation for such odd fixations and what could be going on inside his head. Does he think?

When we asked ourselves this question Neil used to joke that Gabriel reminded him of a story about Mulla Nasreddin, a Sufi wise-fool: In the bazaar, Mulla saw a crowd gathered around a small bird offering big prices for it.

'No doubt the price of birds and fowls has gone up,' Mulla thought to himself. He went home and, after some chase, succeeded in catching his old turkey. In the bazaar they offered only two silver coins for the turkey.

'It's not fair,' Mulla said. 'My turkey is several times as big as that bird auctioned at so many gold pieces.'

'But that bird was a parakeet; it talks.'

Mulla took a glance at the turkey dozing in his arms. 'Mine thinks,' he said.

So we had another name for our son, Mulla's Turkey. And just to illustrate what an apt name it is, this morning he spent about twenty minutes trying to pull his short T-shirt sleeves down to the wrist beneath his jumper. They must have been teaching him at school to pull his sleeves down, perhaps when he puts his coat on, but haven't differentiated between short and long sleeves. He got more and more frantic with frustration at the impossibility of it. As soon as he succeeded in pulling one sleeve down, the moment he turned his attention to the other the first disappeared up his arm again – which would have been funny had he not got so upset.

A lot of the teaching at school is done 'hand over hand'. For children to whom language presents such problems and who do not, cannot, imitate movements (though oddly, those who are echolalic are only too skilled at imitating speech), it is necessary to guide them through actions – moving their limbs, hands or even jaws in some cases, for them. (Maybe there is a connection with Facilitated Communication here. Therese Joliffe writes too: 'I always feel I can understand things better through my fingers.') So we take Gabriel's knife and place it in his hand, his index finger lying along the top of the blade. He doesn't help. He doesn't grasp the knife and his hand is as limp as a dead fish. His finger slips off the knife, twice, three times, and you try to hold it in position with your own hand as you spread a piece of bread. He's completely uninterested, doesn't seem particularly motivated by the prospect of a nice peanut butter sandwich and his attention has evaporated in seconds. At 16 his self-help skills are lamentably limited, but we all – and especially those dedicated teachers and welfare assistants at school – keep on trying. We have to teach our children the most fundamental skills: waving goodbye, pointing, telling left shoe from right, brushing hair; not one of which, I might add, has been mastered by Mulla's Turkey. Progress is slow, so slow.

Progress is slow elsewhere too. Letters have gone back and forth concerning the occupational therapist's request to social services to look into a way to keep Gabriel off the roof. At this rate he will have left home before anything has been done, though of course there will be visits home, so there will still be a need for Preventative Measures. Another area for concern is Gabriel's epilepsy. It is now six months since he started on anti-convulsant medication and overall there has been little change. Various drugs and cocktails of drugs – a little more of this one and less of that, phase this one out and try that one, double that dose and halve the other, and so on – have not had any significant effect. He still has fits more or less as frequently as ever and is becoming more and more awkward about taking the drugs. Their principal effect as far as I can see has been to slow him down a bit, but although that might seem a plus in Gabriel's case I am not entirely convinced it's a good thing. It's true there is less manic activity (though that has by no means disappeared) but at the same time some of the sparkle seems to have gone out of him – and his teachers have noticed it too.

Meanwhile Christmas is hurtling towards us. 'Are you spending Christmas at home?' people ask, as if we had any choice. There being no respite over the holiday, Gabriel has always spent Christmas with us. And so he should, you might think. We think so too – though let's not be sentimental. I'm sure we – *I* – would consider sending him to The Haven if it were open, since he does limit us and, one has to say, it probably wouldn't matter to him where he spent Christmas. He doesn't know it's Christmas. Not really. As a family we have spent some Christmases apart because of the difficulties of visiting with him, especially for an overnight stay. (By the same token Gabriel sometimes does us a favour, providing a cast iron excuse for turning down unsolicited invitations or for being unable to attend tedious functions. We can always blame him.)

But I don't want it to sound grim, it's simply how it is. Gabriel is much easier on home ground so we celebrate at home. Most years we have people to stay, but this year it will just be we four, and of course this first Christmas without Neil will be particularly poignant. Otherwise how it all goes will mostly depend on Gabriel and I hope we will be spared any dramas.

We haven't had a tree in recent years because of you-know-who, strands of tinsel making interesting twirlers and the too-fragile baubles with their shiny reflections making attractive playthings. How could he resist them? He couldn't of course, and rather than get stressed over a denuded tree and broken decorations it was simpler to do without. This year though it's time for a change and, hoping Gabriel has matured a little, I've decided to risk one.

Our Wild Boy doesn't really understand or care about presents, but I have bought him A New Coat. I know he will refuse to put it on and I shall have to hide the old one – his present comforter and carapace – before he will accept it. From then on we will have difficulty in parting him from it. Besides the coat I have bought him a ball of string (he keeps taking mine out of the desk drawer and tangling it), a packet of balloons and some party poppers as well as a plentiful supply of his favourite sweets. There is a present from school too – a 'psychedelic' object consisting of coloured oil and water in a plastic container – which I'm sure has been chosen with great thought. All in all a modest collection, but he doesn't care and – I'm not being cynical – he will probably enjoy playing with the wrapping as much as the contents.

Christmas Eve

The Lad must have had a fit last night as he was out for the count all morning giving me time to put the finishing touches to the decorations and do up some last-minute wrapping. I kept a couple of strands of tinsel to one side so the tree would not be stripped too promptly and left some pieces of tissue paper around should Gabriel feel in a shredding mood. I wondered if pandering to his fixations was taking the easy way out – *that* should keep him quiet – or was it a simple desire to give him what he likes best. The fact is, he cannot be forced to give up fiddling (threads, leaves, scraps of paper are always to hand) and who knows we might even make things worse by trying. His passionate twiddling is his Prozac and protection; it is how he survives his changing moods and circumstances. He needs it and, what the hell, it's Christmas and I'm going to indulge him.

In the afternoon I placed candles around the room and lit them. Gabriel had fun blowing them out as fast as I lit them but left the tree alone and after a while left the candles to burn. It looked cosy and festive and the lovely piney scent of the tree filled the room and I gave him a tin of biscuits the taxi driver had bought him. 'They're for you,' I told him, 'you can eat as many as you like.' Just then a friend called with her 5-year-old son. I tried to persuade Gabriel to let Michael have one of the biscuits, but he was fiercely possessive of them and put the lid on firmly every time I went near him. He has no concept of sharing (something which is very difficult to teach a rampant egotist) and when eventually I managed to extricate one and give it to the little boy he rushed over and snatched it back. Michael was torn between fascination and fear of this, as he saw it, strange and naughty boy and had to be consoled with some sweets. Later The Lad and I passed the evening together listening to music as the other two were out having fun. I'd like to go out and have fun too but I'm confined to base.

Christmas Day

Well, not too bad. No moods, no fits, no escapes. Gabriel quite sleepy during the day and refused a bracing Christmas walk, though came to for roast turkey and demolished enough for three. Didn't take a lot of notice of his presents though once brought me a spoon to cut him a length of string. Brains of Britain! I tried to teach him to pull the party poppers. I thought he would like the bang and all the paper streamers. Hand over hand, I tried time after time, but his fingers could have been made of jelly and he just couldn't be bothered. He preferred to be left alone to mess about in his usual fashion. Later some friends of the boys came to pass the evening with us. Gabriel always seems to enjoy having visitors and he stood near them with his string stealing secret peeps at them while ostensibly ignoring them. One of them obligingly blew up the balloons and let them go zig-zagging madly across the room or pulled the necks to make them squeak and parp – just the sort of thing he loves – and after the roast turkey provided the high point of his day.

To bed at one-thirty. Whacked. Me, that is.

Boxing Day

We have a good laugh remembering the year Gabriel managed to slip unnoticed out of the back door while everyone was ensconced in front of the television. Instant panic – he'd had at least half an hour's start on us and it was 9 o'clock at night. After ringing the police ('small boy aged 13 but looks 10, red slippers and jogging bottoms, can't speak, no road sense, could be anywhere') we and the visiting cousins all fanned out into the dark leaving Jacob to man the phone. The search party returned empty handed, but soon a call from the police told us they had been contacted by the publican from *The Crystal Palace*, a pub a short distance along the towpath. A strange young lad, in slippers and dripping wet (he must have either fallen or jumped in the canal on the way) had entered the bar, was helping himself to the crisps and customers' beers, and wouldn't stop…

No such adventures this year thankfully, in fact he spent most of the day in his room. When at one point I went to investigate I found him sitting head in hands and as I approached he started to cry – real tears. I sat beside him and tried to comfort him, but he continued to sob heart-rendingly as the tears fell. Then he got up, pushed me out of the room and closed the door. What was wrong? What could I do? What could anyone do? I may joke and call Gabriel Mulla's Turkey, but turkeys don't cry and the tears were evidence of deep human emotion. Whether they were tears from feelings of loss, frustration, alienation, existential angst – or none of those – he was the picture of misery and aloneness, the characteristic aloneness of autism. Yet Gabriel possesses an enviable resilience and is rarely downcast for long. A short time later his animal nature reasserted itself. I was picking over the turkey for dinner when he tore into the kitchen, took a handful of gristle and bone intended for the dog, stuffed it in his mouth and crunched up the lot, then scooped water out of the dog's dish to wash it all own. Ugh!

New Year

Gabriel is off to The Haven for three nights while we go and spend time with my family in Dorset. We were lucky this year to be allocated time over New Year. Exhausted from Christmas and its aftermath I can't wait to see the back of Son Number Two. (Nothing personal Gabriel, but I need to flap my wings.) Perhaps it's mutual and he will enjoy the different atmosphere and company, but I don't really care. I'm desperate for a break and a chance to renew my energy. Thank heavens again for respite.

The year having turned, we returned home and soon it was back to school and the assessment at the college coming up the following week. One of the welfare assistants from school took him for the day and reported that all passed without incident, though Gabriel had not participated in any activities, had not eaten and had spent most of his time fiddling in a corner. A week later the college authorities suggested he spent another day there for further observation and, although I did my best to stifle them, alarm bells started to ring.

Beginning February

Well, I should have prepared myself for the worst. I was stupid to expect things to go smoothly – and they haven't. I received a letter today telling me that they feel the college is *not* a suitable place for Gabriel, their principal worry being security. This is of course a valid point, for although the unit for autistic students was surrounded by a high fence the wider surroundings were not (but then how did they deal with the other autistic students who presumably also needed a high level of supervision?). I have to admit I am deeply disappointed to be landed back on square one after all these months. As for the social worker, she is furious at the inefficiency and the way we have been messed around for so long. Surely these processes could be speeded up a bit? A meeting is scheduled at school next week to decide on the next move.

Meanwhile the Wild Boy has not been idle. Two nights ago he surpassed himself and what I had been dreading for months finally happened – he actually went *through* the neighbours' roof.

Having gone up to his room after school he managed to push out a pane of double glazing (which fell on the tiles of our extension below breaking three of them), then squeezed out of the very small opening and across to the neighbours' extension roof. This time his weight was too much or the roof had become weakened by his regular forays up there, so he went straight through it. Needless to say elderly Mr and Mrs Smith were none too pleased to be sitting quietly eating their evening meal when a crash in the next room alerted them to the disaster. I was summoned to survey the damage and remove the culprit. He was sitting, unhurt and twiddling, in an armchair into which he had fallen (trust him!) surrounded by a sprinkling of polystyrene ceiling tiles and other debris. Fortunately the damage was limited to the roof itself. He hadn't landed on the television set or on the nearby glass table displaying precious breakables and potted plants. For once in his life, I think he realised he had gone too far. Looking ever so slightly chastened as I berated him, he blinked rapidly into the middle distance (a warding off strategy), but obeyed me when I told him to get up and go back home. It was dark and the rain was bucketing down and another neighbour (a builder) had to be called in to cover the gaping hole with some lead and a tarpaulin. What a trial he is. I shall hardly be able to look the Smiths in the face after this.

Still every cloud has a silver lining. Someone from social services was due to come the very next day to assess the need for Preventative Measures and was able to see that I hadn't been exaggerating. Our hero couldn't have timed it better. What's more the neighbours had been planning to replace said roof for some months; Neil had actually helped them get the materials and was to do it for them the very week he lost his life. As a result their son had promised to do it for them in the spring. So I suppose it could have been worse.

I guess he just can't help being mischievous. He reminds me of a boy with Asperger's syndrome I saw on TV, who after some misdemeanour and as a reminder was reciting to his Mum's video camera, 'I must not do it again, I must not do it again, I must not do it again, I must not...' Then finished with a big grin: 'But, I probably will.' Many people with autism seem to have an irrepressible talent for mischief or, as Temple Grandin put it, 'unique and creative ways of being naughty'.

We have had the meeting at school and I have arranged to check out some other places. I have learnt of an organisation which has half a dozen homes for adults with learning disabilities, all of them within 50 miles of here. Most of them house six to eight residents and are large converted family homes. But are they suitable and do they have vacancies? Gabriel's teacher offers to accompany me and give her opinion. (I must put on record here the assistance I have received from the school and from Gabriel's social worker. They have made tireless efforts to help and support, as in fact have most of the front-line professionals. It's the bureaucrats that cause most of the problems.)

It is nearly March and tonight Gabriel was in full wind-up mode. He poured a bottle of cleaner down the sink and a bottle of lemon squash over the kitchen floor. Kept turning the TV off while we were trying to watch something or flicked lights on and off (he often seems to resent us watching the small amount of television that we indulge in), sat on top of the sitting-room door for an hour, dipped endless tissues in the dog's water and shredded them throughout the house, took cake and crumbled it in bath, and so on. In short, he really enjoyed himself this evening.

'You'll miss him when he leaves,' say my friends. Will I? Will I miss an evening like last night? Or calamities like the neighbours' roof? Will I miss BMs and bottoms, sleepless nights and Big Moods? I don't think so. But will my life seem empty without my wild boy there to keep me busy? The relationship with a handicapped child is often a symbiotic one and while we as parents might on the one hand resent the demands made on us, we can also find ourselves *needing to be needed*. One can build an identity on the foundations of the disabled one and sometimes be reluctant to let go of it.

The problem is that we cannot separate Gabriel from the life he forces us to live and however much I may miss *him* – and of course I will – for myself, I cannot deny that the vision of a life unfettered by the demands he imposes on me, not having to be home to meet the taxi every afternoon, being able to socialise in the evenings and at weekends and pursue my own interests, is a prospect that fills me with pleasure.

17

A free spirit

April

With Gabriel's teacher I have been to see a selection of homes. They are within easy reach of here but I am a bit nervous about them all being situated in or on the outskirts of busy towns. The organisation which owns them seems to have made a genuine effort to make them as homely as possible – they're quite cosy and attractive – but as most of them are converted family homes they have limited space both indoors and out. They are willing to offer Gabriel a place and I am seriously considering it, though there is again the problem of his age. Special permission will be needed to accept him as he will be under 18. This could take weeks or, more realistically, months to arrange and in the meantime the one available place could be taken. Every day the place is empty means the organisation is losing money; they need to fill spaces as quickly as possible. Meanwhile the careers officer has heard of a new home recently set up for especially difficult clients. This sounds more like it, though it is some distance away, and the school Head and I make an appointment to visit there the next time Gabriel is at The Haven.

The home, or college so-called, ludicrous as that may strike some readers, is 130 miles away and is a large old rectory on the edge of a small village, with extensive grounds all surrounded by a high fence. (Good, good.) It includes classrooms for the 20 or so students during term time where they continue to be taught – well, whatever they can be taught: to make a piece of toast, dry the dishes, do a jigsaw puzzle, learn to sign 'biscuit' and so on. Classes are not compulsory and students have the right not to attend. Every resident has his or her own bedroom and bathroom (there's luxury for you), the staffing level is high. The Principal seems trustworthy and good hearted and at the end of our tour is prepared to offer Gabriel a place, which the Head urges me to accept. However, it is not only the distance which makes me hesitate but the fact that being a college the students have to leave at age 25, when I shall have to start looking all over again. (That might seem a long way off at the moment but experience has shown me that the day will arrive all too soon.) But I'm tempted and we agree that someone from the college will come to see Gabriel at school to further assess his suitability.

Now I am between a rock and a hard place.

End-April

I phoned social services again and literally cried tears of rage, frustration and self-pity. Gabriel is constantly making attempts to get up the drainpipe now that spring is here and he spends more time outside. I am getting desperate. When will they decide about the money for the preventative measures? How long does it take? This has been going on since last year! But it all falls on deaf ears, and I'm nothing but a number.

A man who has eaten cannot put himself in the place of one who is hungry.

Another birthday has been and gone and now Gabriel is 17 and on the verge of leaving home. I have to remind myself that he is no longer a child. It is true he looks young for his age, but physically he is turning into a young man and, having always been somewhat hirsute, he already has a moustache, a light beard and amazingly hairy legs. His voice has deepened and my beautiful little boy has become a gangling teenager, incipient acne and all, yet one who needs all the care and protection one gives to a small child. He wears nappies (must remember to call them pads), but now has pubic hair. I still have to hold his hand or arm when we cross the street, although he is now a head taller than I am and has a beard. I can't carry on referring to him as a boy or child. Sometimes one of our old names for him – Boysie – slips out and although I am sure he doesn't give two hoots what we call him if I'm not careful I'll find myself in a timewarp.

May

The Deputy Head of the college has been to see Gabriel at school. I was there too. The prospective student behaved true to form, the offer of a place was repeated and I accepted it. I can't afford to dither and the other place might never come through. Now things are starting to move at a rapid pace. I am to take Gabriel to the college next week to let him have a look at it and he should move in soon after.

One of the welfare assistants from school drives me and Gabriel to the college for our visit and we are able to have a good look round. Gabriel's room is to be in a new wing which is nearing completion and we point out that the windows are not secure enough for this student. He'll be out of them in a flash. The Deputy Head who is accompanying us makes a note of this. The room is bare containing only a minimum of furniture (many residents cannot be trusted not to pull down curtains) and Gabriel lies stomach down on the bedside mat and begins humping it while the Deputy remarks that besides sleeping the students use their rooms for – with a wry smile and a glance at the heaving body at his feet – 'leisure activity'.

I ask about their attitude to medication as we have, by general consent, now taken Gabriel off the anti-convulsants, and I am assured that they will abide by that decision at least for the time being. The emphasis is on involving parents as far as possible in all such decisions. One thing I am pleased to note is that there are as many male staff as female – unlike at school or The Haven – as I feel Gabriel needs and would respect some firm masculine presence. It is easy for him to take advantage of the physically weaker sex. We discuss food, clothes, outings, toiletting, the college curriculum and Gabriel's abilities and disabilities and it is agreed he will move in sometime in July.

I am never sure if it is right to talk about Son Number Two in his presence. It presumes he doesn't understand (and therefore doesn't matter). Yet we often do it – have to at times like this – and today I hope he is gathering some inkling of our plans for his future and it won't come as a complete shock when we bring him back ready to move in. It's impossible to tell though. He seems happy enough as we go round the building but refuses the lunch that is prepared for us. Back home we had a bad evening when he went berserk with some black paint he managed to get hold of and had a lively night – all night. It wasn't necessarily connected, it happens all the time, but was just another reminder why he is going to the college.

End of June

At last! The builders came yesterday – exactly three weeks before Gabriel is due to leave home – and put a barrier all round the edge of the extension that he couldn't get a grip of or haul himself over. It's not a very aesthetic addition but as long as it works I shall be happy and I can now relax when he roams in the garden.

The last few weeks seem to have flown by and suddenly D-day – departure day, 16 July – has arrived. There was a farewell party and presents from school last week and The Haven also gave him a send-off. I have been talking to him about going away and showing him what I have packed. There are photographs of all of us and pictures for the wall, a tape-player (to be used under supervision of course) and his brothers have taped some familiar music. There is a bag of his favourite twirlers and – to make the message clearer – his duvet. Whether any of this has gone in I can't tell; Mulla's Turkey remains inscrutable and as we all drive north he carries on as usual. Fiddle, fiddle, fiddle in the back of the car all the way to the college. A carer greets us at the door and takes us to Gabriel's room and Jacob wrinkles his nose at the institutional smell while Christian mutters about the institutional decor – but I'm used to it by now and I truly don't think it matters to Gabriel. We unpack his bags and put his clothes away in the wardrobe and his duvet on the bed, all the while talking about his nice new room and telling him he'll soon settle in. I give him some sweets and a twirler but I don't want to linger, don't want him to grab my arm and take me to the front door – his way of telling me he wants to leave. In fact I don't even want to say goodbye for fear it will provoke a scene. Miming my intention to the carer who is about to follow Gabriel into the bathroom where he is testing the taps, we take our chance to slip quickly and unobtrusively out of the room. Before leaving the building we see another member of staff who promises to telephone me later about the new student and tells me not to worry.

My new life – and his – is about to begin. Returning home feels very strange and the house seems emptier and quieter than usual when he is away. I pick up a stray shoelace lying on the stairs, wipe some sticky handprints off the kitchen wall and unscrew and open wide the windows in Gabriel's room to let out its characteristic whiff of the stable. Later that evening I notice a few nicks have been taken out of the large, fleshy leaves of a succulent houseplant. Gabriel has left his mark.

I've been advised that it is better not to see the new student for at least a month, that the longer he has to settle in before renewing contact the better, though I can ring at any time to ask about him and the college will telephone once a week anyway to keep me informed. 'Don't worry,' I tell myself. 'He'll be all right,' and I smile each time I notice the mutilated leaves of my houseplant. At other moments my picture of him is so lonely and forlorn that I feel an ache of helplessness: 'Will they understand him? Does he miss us?' and the house echoes emptily in reply. Eventually he will have his own personal tutor who will be responsible for keeping in touch, but a tutor is not appointed until student and staff have got to know each other, giving time for personal bonds to develop and the chance to match carers and students as happily as possible.

Like ducks into water we slip into our new lives. Being financially worse off with Gabriel's departure I go back to work. Time takes on a different dimension and I luxuriate in long uninterrupted evenings and weekends. We linger and talk over our meals and I wonder how I ever managed to fit anything in when he was at home. Where did I find the time or energy to read a book or to just sit and think? And oh how I relish wallowing in the bath without having one ear cocked for calamity. When Gabriel returns it all comes back to me.

By the end of his first year at college we have settled into a routine as far as visits are concerned. Visiting him there for the day soon proved unsatisfactory. He wanted to come home. I couldn't really take him out anywhere, though we sometimes went for a walk, and a few hours spent sitting around the college didn't appeal. So now he always comes to us and every six or seven weeks spends three or four nights in his second home. I find that's my limit. I have already got out of the habit of still being on the go at midnight or later, changing pads. I have already forgotten about the hard work and the demands on my patience, energy and attention and each time he comes home I have to prepare myself, psyche myself up.

On the drive up to college and as the sky opens up over the flat Lincolnshire landscape, as the handsome spire of the church adjoining the college becomes visible, I gradually endeavour to squeeze back into my old skin. I am filled with a mixture of apprehension and anticipation; the former in case I can't cope or something horrendous happens during the following days, the latter because I am looking forward to seeing that big grin of recognition.

'But does he *know* you?' some people ask me. Of course he knows me! I don't suppose for one moment that he knows me as his mother, that he has any conception of the word 'mother', but he recognises me as someone who cares for him and provides for him and when I appear he is (nearly always) pleased to see me. I'm sure he's equally pleased because he knows it means a visit home; it means his favourite foods (I did remember to get that extra jar of peanut butter, didn't I? And the bag of Maltesers?); familiar music; familiar faces, smells, walks and surroundings. Nevertheless I'm still gratified if I get a smile, even if I only represent the peanut butter waiting for him in the kitchen cupboard.

He always looks clean and well-cared for and his bag is packed and ready. Gabriel can make the connection – packed bag equals home visit. While a member of staff hands me a bag of pads the Lad is already tugging at my sleeve and heading for the door, so wasting no time we set off immediately. In the car I talk to him a bit and pat his hand, but he pushes mine away and shuts his eyes and I put on a tape. Back home it's as if he's never been away. He heads straight for the sugar jar and eats all the sugar, he finds the washing-up liquid and squirts it on the floor (my fault, I forgot to hide it), then pulls me to the hi-fi. He finds his twirlers and dashes into the garden where he squints up at the roof undecided whether to try and scale the wire barrier or to come in and ransack the cupboards for biscuits. Thankfully he settles for the biscuits and after emptying the tin (I let him, he's on holiday), he then disappears upstairs to familiarise himself with the old place and perhaps just try the windows (which have all been tightly secured in preparation for the visit – bad luck, Gabriel). Yet after going through his little repertoire, including later stripping off and running outside for some leaves, he seems happy just to be here, lazing around the living room enjoying the home routine and being the guest of honour.

I unpack his bag and find his new tutor has bought him jeans and button-up shirts and sigh with irritation. What is the point of buying Gabriel jeans? He cannot manage zips and buttons. They only make him a prisoner in his own clothes and will surely make any toilet training more difficult if ever attempted. Jeans don't look that great over a pad either and in order to accommodate one they have to be so big they need a belt, or to be hitched up endlessly if they are not to end up with the crutch between the knees. I guess this is an attempt at 'normalisation,' but is it a useful one?

Clothing is a difficult area for parents and when, before Gabriel left for college, I asked one mother what happened about clothes when children left home she told me she didn't know of a single parent who was happy about handing over the clothes buying to someone else. We don't mind handing over the bottom wiping, but perhaps for many of us the way we dressed our sons and daughters was one of the ways we enjoyed caring for them and could show we were proud of them. Naturally we also dress them according to our own tastes and if we like natural fibres, say, we don't want them coming home in crimplene. (A later tutor wrote that he was intending to buy Gabriel some new clothes, adding that he was 'a young man who takes a pride in his appearance'. We had a good laugh at this piece of fantasy and seeing him on his next visit home with his boxer shorts on top of his trousers, Christian commented, 'Hmm, very proud.')

Yet although the clothing problem is relatively insignificant (and the jeans vs. jogging bottoms difference was easily resolved), the truth is that we are reluctant to relinquish some of our responsibilities. In fact it is galling as well as extremely frustrating to have to accept that we actually have no real say in how our children are treated once they have left home and moved into residential care. We no longer have any rights or official responsibilities regarding these people, our children. For example, if 'they' decide that a client would benefit from a particular drug, for whatever reason, then there is very little the parent can do about it. If it is decided that 'Michael' has been a bit difficult lately and that tranquillisers might help and if after a while his mother thinks they are having a deleterious effect on him, then tough. (Even if it is admitted that perhaps the drug is causing some unwanted symptoms, then the solution is not to take Michael off the drug, but rather to give him more, or add another.) As for laxatives and antibiotics in my opinion they are prescribed far too freely. It's true that the modern way is to talk about shared care and consultation, but it just ain't like that when it comes right down to it.

But I'm not knocking the college or other places like it. I understand that their first responsibility is to the clients in their care, and besides they don't make all the rules. The truth is that care for people with learning difficulties – especially those like Gabriel – has improved immeasurably in recent years and cannot be denied. Gone are the days when such people would have been left to vegetate in some large institution, many of them probably on something to keep them quiet, and with nothing to look forward to but a coach trip to Southend once a year. Since Gabriel has been in residential care he has enjoyed a wider range of activities than he ever would at home: barbecues and horse-riding, parties and regular outings every week, including trips to the local pub. Yes, he does go there after all, though not for darts but a coke and packet of crisps in the garden. Plus there is always food if he is hungry, music if he wants to listen to it, a sensory room, television, plenty of clean clothes, baths and so on –

with always someone on hand to see to his needs. Of course this service does not come cheap – multiply by four or five what it costs to keep your Granny in a home and you will have some idea of the cost. (When I heard how much I joked, 'Just give me half of that and he can stay at home.' I could then afford to employ someone full-time to help me with him *and* save tax-payers' money.)

But the most important point is that attitudes have changed and the students (who, incidentally, are not all autistic) are treated with a tremendous amount of affection and respect by those who look after them. There is a genuine desire to understand them and their difficulties, to help them make whatever progress they are capable of and to enrich their lives.

Meanwhile our visit goes fairly smoothly and I can enjoy Gabriel's company. We listen to music I haven't heard for a while. I potter about while he fiddles contentedly and I'm happy to see him tuck into a dish I have prepared specially for him. It's true he invariably manages to stay awake at least one night when he is home and getting him to bed, no matter how late I leave it, continues to stretch my patience. There's the mess that magically materialises within minutes of his arrival and the keys, but as I so often remind myself, he can't help it and he really does seem to enjoy his visits. On the other hand, when it is time to return to college (now he has settled in) he is eager to go and when we arrive there he disappears into the building without a backward glance. I needn't worry that he misses us then and I doubt that he has any sense of time, so that when we meet again he doesn't know if six days or six months have passed since he last saw me.

Between visits I get a weekly phone call – a rundown of his BMs (still can't forget about them) and seizures (or them), outings and behaviour.

'Gabriel's been fine. Really good – he even shared a bag of crisps with another student this afternoon. Just a bit of SIB yesterday.'

'SIB?'

'Self Injurious Behaviour.'

'Oh, right.'

'Nothing serious though. He's fine.'

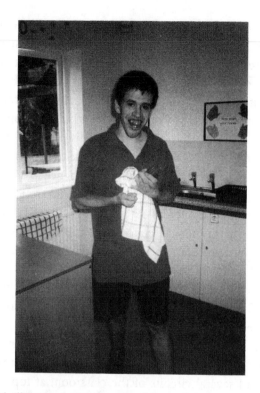

At college – 'thrilled when he dried up a cup!'

College student – one eye still focused way off. Not really paying attention to threading cotton reels

And so he is. After four years at college now he continues to become more mature and stable and the wild child of the past is rarely in evidence. The really bad moods and the SIB have almost disappeared and the desire to escape has diminished. Not that I would trust him – he did get out of his bedroom window in the middle of the night and try to climb into the neighbour's bedroom window on one visit – but these escapades are getting further apart. His present personal tutor (who was so keen to be Gabriel's tutor that he refused to take on any other student but preferred to wait until the chance to take on Gabriel arose) frequently assures me that his charge is 'no trouble' compared to some of the students. He and other members of staff often mention how much Gabriel is appreciated for his 'sense of humour', by which they mean his mischievous and provocative way of interacting with those around him and his gleeful grin.

The aims of his teachers are still modest. At his last six-monthly review one future objective was 'to access a shop'. (This after *four years*.) Apparently he enjoys his time in the classroom and recently has taken an interest in drying up (!). On one occasion his teacher reported he 'successfully dried one cup and was so thrilled with himself he did several circuits of the classroom at top speed'. Not exactly a breakthrough, but remember it's all relative. They continue in trying to develop his communication skills which remain 'needs led' and although he now relates better to others, especially some favourite people, he still 'tends to enjoy his own company more than the company of others'. Nevertheless, teachers and care staff emphasise that 'Gabriel is a very popular student'.

It goes without saying that my son will need to be looked after for the rest of his life (and that where I live will depend on where he lives. I won't want to be making a similar journey when I'm 80). Many things haven't changed: his carers have had little success so far in getting him out of pads and the epileptic fits continue to be of great concern. (He is back on anti-convulsant drugs and has been hospitalised several times on account of his epilepsy since he left home.)

But while Gabriel will always be dependent on others for his physical and material needs his autism makes him independent in a way that most of us are not. He is independent in that he does not need our admiration or good opinion, does not need to be valued by others or even liked – as long as he has done no harm of course. Sometimes I feel woefully redundant when I go to collect him and he doesn't seem that bothered about seeing me or coming home. Gabriel is his own person, a 'free spirit' as one teacher described him years ago, who lives in his own world and only chooses to join ours on his own terms. We have to respect him for that.

Finally, the reader would be forgiven for hoping perhaps, as I also once did, for some unexpected turn of events – a wonder drug or a new therapy and therefore a new Gabriel. It hasn't happened, but is that to say his is a meaningless life and not worth the telling? He is as helpless as ever and this is certainly not a success story in the conventional sense, but it is true nonetheless that over the years the Wild Boy has calmed down, has matured, is generally happy and popular. These are not mean achievements; they are ones of which anyone could be justifiably proud. Moreover Gabriel's achievements do not relate only to himself but also to the impact he has had on others. He has touched the lives and holds a real place in the affections of so many – from taxi drivers to kitchen staff. He has taught family, carers and teachers patience, tolerance, different perspectives and new ways of looking at others and themselves. Most of all – and perhaps in the scheme of things this is the role of such people as Gabriel – he has generated an enormous amount of unconditional love. And no doubt will continue to do so.

When I think back to that conversation years ago when I was asked if I felt blessed to have a child like Gabriel I couldn't imagine that anyone would feel like that. Now, I think I have a small idea of what that means and I'm grateful.

List of Quotations

p.27 'Sweet are the uses of adversity'. Shakespeare, *As You Like It*.

p.42 'For me one of the most difficult aspects...' *Communication* (1993) Spring.

p.42 'Responding with an indirect...' Donna Williams (1992) *Nobody Nowhere*. New York: Doubleday, p.196.

p.48 'I tried to remember...' Donna Williams (1994) *Somebody Somewhere*. London: Corgi, p.91.

p.65 'that the precipitating factor...' Bruno Bettelheim (1967) *The Empty Fortress: Infantile Autism and the Birth of the Self*. New York: The Free Press, p.125.

p.82 'Just when you are relieved...' *Communication* (1992) June, p.7.

p.900 'Children with autistic conditions... feelings.' Lorna Wing (1996) *The Autistic Spectrum*. London: Constable, p.57.

p.90 'It is life as the only person...' Donna Williams (1992) *Good Housekeeping*, May.

p.119 'Generally, brothers and sisters...' *Communication* (1990), March, p.11.

p.127 'mobile home'. Donna Williams (1992) *Nobody Nowhere*. New York: Doubleday, p.65.

p.132 'I found him seated...' Harlan Lane (1977) *The Wild Boy of Aveyron*. London: George Allen & Unwin, p.7.

p.133 'Once back at home...' (ibid.) p.8.

p.134 'something extraordinary...' (ibid.) p.9.

p.135 'annoyed him greatly.' (ibid.) p.10.

p.135 'nothing can console...' (ibid.) p.18.

p.135 'a child cut off...' (ibid.) p.18.

p.135 'taken a single step...' (ibid.) p.18.

p.137 'his desires do not exceed...' (ibid.) p38–39.

p.137 'When kissed he does not notice...' (ibid.) p.42.

p.137 'If he is thwarted...' (ibid.) p.42.

p.137 'is much inclined to theft...' (ibid.) p.43.

p.137 'children of his own age...' (ibid.) p.42.

p.137 'He likes solitude a great deal...' (ibid.) p.43.

p.137 'many believed that the education...' (ibid.) p.53.

p.138 'highly circumscribed...' (ibid.) p.59.

p.138–139 'Madame Recamier... scene so strikingly contrasted.' (ibid.) pp.108–109.

p.139 'If he is in town...' (ibid.) p.115.

p.140 'the most powerful methods...' (ibid.) p.159.

p.140 'fearful and half wild.' (ibid.) p.167.

p.141 'like a squirrel' and 'animal fashion...' Percy C. Birtchnell (1972) *A Short History of Berkhamsted*. The Book Stack, p.111.

p.141 'royalty, novelists...' (ibid.) p.11.

p.141   'the first autistic hero...' Thelma Grove (1988) *Communication*, March.

p.141   'unusual pet'. Percy C. Birtchnell (1972) *A Short History of Berkhamsted.* The Book Stack, p.111.

p.141   'incapable of speaking...' (ibid.) p.111.

p.2   'as a different species' Elisa Segrave (1996) *The London Review of Books,* 17 October.

p.145   'the emotion circuit's...' Oliver Sacks (1995) *An Anthropologist on Mars.* London: Picador, p.273.

p.147   'I could read them...' Donna Williams (1992) *Nobody Nowhere.* New York: Doubleday, p.38.

p.147   'bewildered', 'never knew...' Temple Grandin. In Oliver Sacks *An Anthropologist on Mars.* London: Picador, p.247.

p.48   'sensory hell.' Donna Williams (1994) *Somebody Somewhere.* London: Corgi, p.23.

p.148   'painfulness of sounds...' Donna Williams (1992) *Nobody Nowhere.* New York: Doubleday, p.168.

p.148   'unintelligible mass...' (ibid.) p.176.

p.148   'Loud noise...' Temple Grandin (1989) *Communication*, December.

p.149   'quietness was being disturbed.' Therese Jolliffe (1992) *Communication,* December.

p.149   'meaning deaf', 'In terms...' Donna Williams (1994) *Somebody Somewhere.* London: Corgi, p.48.

p.149   'When I was very young...' Therese Jolliffe (1992) *Communication,* December.

p.149   'I find it as difficult to understand...' (ibid.).

p.149   'the air was full of spots...' Donna Williams (1992) *Nobody Nowhere.* New York: Doubleday, p.3.

p.149   'I have since learned...' (ibid.) p.9.

p.149   'tracing every...' Donna Williams (1994) *Somebody Somewhere.* London: Corgi, p.112.

p.149   'the beautiful side...' (ibid.) p.113.

p.149   'tortured by sharp white...' (ibid.) p.74.

p.6   'People do not appreciate...' Therese Jolliffe (1992) *Communication,* December.

p.150   'when they are unaware of it' (ibid.)

p.150   'One was to look straight...' Donna Williams (1992) *Nobody Nowhere.* New York: Doubleday, p.173.

p.150   'It is almost as bad...' Therese Jolliffe (1992) *Communication,* December.

p.150   'Dr M was...' Donna Williams (1994) *Somebody Somewhere.* London: Corgi, p.121.

p.150   'I pulled away...' Temple Grandin (1989) *Communication,* December.

p.151   'He touched my hair...' Donna Williams (1992) *Nobody Nowhere.* New York: Doubleday, p.159.

p.151   'It was the threat...' (ibid.) p.116.

p.151   'the comforting feeling...' Temple Grandin (1989) *Communication,* December.

p.151   'Abnormalities of the cerebellum...' (ibid.).

p.151 'it would be beneficial...' (ibid.).

p.151 'craving', 'squeeze machine'. (ibid.).

p.152 'I used to have...' *Communication*, December 1989.

p.153 'I can recall it...' Daniel Hill (1997) *Daily Mail*, 13 May.

p.154 'Growing knowledge...' Lorna Wing (1996) *The Autistic Spectrum*. London: Constable, p.22.

p.156 'To me the suffering was terrible...' Therese Jolliffe (1992) *Communication*, December.

p.156 'mainly due to desensitization...' Temple Grandin (1989) *Communication*, December.

p.157 'completely emerged...' *Communication*, spring 1998.

p.158 'This once virtually...' *Communication*, spring 1999.

p.159 'The fact that...' *Communication*, spring 1997.

p.164 'There are many stories...' Lorna Wing (1996) *The Autistic Spectrum*. London: Constable, p.50.

p.164 'funny sensation... bitten.' Donna Williams (1994) *Somebody Somewhere*. London: Corgi, p.27.

p.165 'Many children and adults...' Lorna Wing (1996) *The Autistic Spectrum*. London: Constable, p.108.

p.166 *Alice's Adventures in Wonderland*. Lewis Carroll (1865).

p.173 'Everything I did...' Donna Williams (1992) *Nobody Nowhere*. New York: Doubleday, p.26.

p.186 'Sleep was not...' Donna Williams (1994) *Somebody Somewhere*. London: Corgi, p.6.

p.186 'much of the fervour'. Temple Grandin. In Oliver Sacks (1995) *An Anthropologist on Mars*. London: Picador, p.261.

p.189 Mulla Nasreddin story. In Massud Farzan (1973) *Another Way of Laughter*. New York: Clarke, Irwin, p.23.

p.190 'I always feel...' Therese Jolliffe (1992) *Communication*.

p.196 'unique and creative...' Oliver Sacks (1995) *An Anthropologist on Mars*. London: Picador, p.259.